# The DERBYSHIRE Cook Book

A celebration of the amazing food & drink on our doorstep.
Featuring over 40 stunning recipes.

# FOREWORD

It's strange looking back, but we didn't come to Derbyshire because of where it was, it was more born out of desperation.

Over 35 years ago I was working as a head chef in Germany and my extremely supportive wife, Susan, was expecting our first son. I had grown tired of working for someone else and told Susan I planned to hand my notice in and run my own business.

Our families understandably thought we'd gone mad and in a panic Susan's parents bought a property magazine, which featured a barn in Bakewell, Derbyshire. My son was born on a Friday, I flew on Saturday to the UK, viewed the restaurant and accepted it.

I love cooking; with the same passion as a musician who will never stop playing. And for me Derbyshire has been - and still is – the perfect place to do so.

From the start I implemented my own style of cooking, following the ethos I had learned growing up that if I couldn't make it I wasn't going to serve it – I have always made all the elements of my dishes from scratch in the kitchen.

My menus are a reflection of good quality local produce cooked well, from back in the barn in Bakewell to present day at Rowley's and Michelin-starred Fischer's at Baslow Hall.

There has always been fantastic produce available in Derbyshire, especially beef and lamb, but over the years there has been a profusion of growers and suppliers springing up – think Hartington cheeses, local honey, fresh herbs… it's wonderful really!

I'm also a passionate gardener and between the vegetable garden on the farm where we live and Baslow Hall I grow food for our restaurants including onions, broad beans, spring cabbage and more. In this age of interest in food provenance it's great to see others doing so too.

Derbyshire's food scene is continuing to change and flourish. I believe it will go from strength to strength - and the wonderful places and recipes in this book give a taste of the inspiration to be found here. I'm so glad we took a chance on coming here all those years ago – it has made me what I am.

*Max Fischer*

# CONTENTS

to the following people for making this book possible:

Max Fischer – Fischer's of Baslow Hall

Des Coleman

Roy McFarland

Sam Pinkham – Gem 106

Amy Voce – Gem 106

Sally Pepper – BBC Radio Derby

Zena Hawley – Derby Telegraph

The Derbyshire Cook Book

©2015 Meze Publishing. All rights reserved.

First edition printed in 2015 in the UK.

ISBN: 978-0-9928981-7-5

*Written & Edited by: Adelle Draper*

*Assisted by: Rachel Heward, Emily Beaumont*

*Photography by: Marc Barker, www.marcabarker.com*
*Sam Bowles, www.portraitcollective.com*
*Paul Carroll, www.portraitcollective.com*

*Designed by: Paul Cocker, Samantha Fielding*

*Compiled by: Phil Turner, Amanda Lester*

*Cover art: Luke Prest, www.lukeprest.com*

*Additional photography: Polly Baldwin,*
*James Brown 93ft, Paul Cocker, Miles Doscher,*
*Diane Jarvis VisitEngland, Caroline Bridges,*
*Cactus Images, Matthew Jones, Steve Caddy*

*Contributors: Leah Bradley, Sarah Koriba,*
*Vicky Elwick. Sally Clark, Carl Reid, Linda Robbins,*
*Lesley Draper*

Published by Meze Publishing Limited
Unit 1 Beehive Works
Milton Street
Sheffield S3 7WL
www.mezepublishing.co.uk
Tel: 0114 275 7709
info@mezepublishing.co.uk

My earliest food memories go back to baking with my mum in the kitchen – although the promise of cake bowl 'lickings' was probably what sparked my interest.

My grandma is also a keen baker; my sister and I loved the birthday buns she made, decorated with rainbow hued sweets and sprinkles – no wonder I have a sweet tooth!

Meals were always eaten at the dining table while I was growing up and it was traditional fare. Sunday was a roast dinner, sometimes followed by buttery English muffins or crumpets for tea while watching 'Time Team' on the telly.

My own interest in cooking took off when I went to university and started to experiment – nothing too challenging, but I got the basics down.

More recent inspiration has come from my partner Steve, who's great in the kitchen, and my dad who discovered a late interest in food – regularly creating globally-inspired menus and encouraging me to try new things.

I've been lucky to travel and live abroad, which has broadened my food horizons. From the best hot and sour soup I've ever tasted in Singapore, to chicken schwarma on the roadside in Dubai, melt-in-the-mouth beef and rice in Egypt and the mildest cheese with jam on toast in Norway (not as weird as it sounds). Travel has made me open to trying new things and I've even tasted zebra, kangaroo and python (the latter, believe me, is over-rated!).

I've always kept up with the local food scene thanks to my mum, who has been a newspaper food writer for over 20 years. My interest has led me to run my own PR, social media and copywriting consultancy, specialising in the food and drink sector.

One of my favourite things about writing The Derbyshire Cook Book has been discovering a host of eateries and producers I wasn't previously familiar with – what a fantastic county we live in. I can't wait to get out there and try them all.

Adelle Draper

# Welcome to DERBYSHIRE

Derbyshire's rugged landscape has changed little since cave dwellers first found sanctuary beneath its limestone hills.

But succeeding generations have left their mark on the county and today Derbyshire life is as varied as the natural features that have shaped it – with a food scene to match.

It's a county rich with agriculture and industry, which has in turn spawned a myriad of food producers, restaurateurs, chefs and home cooks, all enjoying what the land has to offer.

Derbyshire is home to classic dishes that are famous around the world, such as Bakewell Pudding and the county's eponymous oatcakes, which have been made and eaten since the 17th century thanks to oat crops thriving in the harsh conditions.

Cheese has long been associated with the county. The first creamery in the UK was reportedly set up by a group of farmers in the village of Longford (Sage Derby was one of the earliest types of cheese to be produced here) and Derbyshire is one of only three counties where Blue Stilton can be made.

These days, Hartington is arguably the centre for production – cheese making has been an important cottage industry there since the late 1800s. Today it produces Dovedale Blue and Buxton Blue as well as Stilton – all big Derbyshire exports.

Production in other areas is now prominent too. For example, cold pressed rapeseed oil is produced at Ashford-in-the-Water, award-winning ice cream is made in Matlock, Hope and Tideswell. A number of farms breed and butcher their own meat, which is then supplied to shops and restaurants across the region and beyond.

And it's not just food and drink – there are acclaimed businesses right on the doorstep designing and manufacturing cutlery, crockery, cookware and kitchen equipment too.

The county is also earning a name as a destination for dining out thanks to a host of independent eateries run by passionate chefs and restaurateurs.

Whether you're looking for handmade produce, or award-winning cooking, Derbyshire has something to offer. Think artisan bakeries, hand-raised pies, organic fruit and vegetables, a whole range of speciality treats and even artisan chocolate.

There are unique cafés, country tea rooms, farm shops, delis, bistros and acclaimed restaurants – one or two boasting a coveted Michelin recommendation.

Breweries too are firmly rooted, with many achieving recognition and even international acclaim for their exciting creative brews. Derby has recently been cited as the real ale capital of Britain by the Lonely Planet Guide – thanks to its abundance of breweries and the diversity of beers available in its pubs and bars.

This book is full to the brim with profiles and recipes from some of these brilliant eateries and producers, highlighting just what a fantastic and unique place Derbyshire is for enjoying food and drink.

Hopefully it will inspire you to seek out some of them or whip up something new in the kitchen.

Cheers!

# *Heart of* DERBYSHIRE

Promoting healthy food is more than just a passing fad; with 'buying local' and provenance being at the very forefront of shoppers minds.

Across the county, hundreds of restaurants, takeaways, cafés and catering services have made pledges to make healthy eating options available in council run initiative 'Heart of Derbyshire'. From vegetables, fruit and wholegrain, to sugar, fat, salt, allergens and portion size pledges, eateries throughout the region are taking steps towards a healthier Derbyshire. You can search for the types of pledges businesses have made on the **www.derbyshire.gov.uk/heartofderbyshire** website, which offers a comprehensive list of venues searchable by type of cuisine and location.

Representative of the vibrant and diverse food and drink scene in Derbyshire, the database includes everything from Italian food to British, Indian, South Asian and Chinese restaurants. For each place you can see the details of the food hygiene rating, opening hours, type of food available and information about pledges they have made to make healthier food available.

With these pledges, venues are taking action and accepting responsibility for the health of their customers, doing their bit to lower the risk of heart disease, type 2 diabetes, strokes and even some cancers.

Simple actions such as offering to grill, poach or steam food instead of frying, using lean meat and low fat ingredients as well as using less salt and offering sugar free options are just some of the ways places throughout the region are being proactive in promoting healthy living.

Some of the names involved in the Heart of Derbyshire scheme include popular haunts such as Ricci's, Zeerah, The Hardwick Inn, Charles Cotton Hotel, Galleon Steakhouse, St Moritz, Hoggs Bistro, The Eating House and Blu Bistro.

So next time you're out and about, look for the gold, silver and bronze Heart of Derbyshire membership stickers, which are determined by the number of pledges the business has made. Happy, healthy eating folks!

# Made in DERBYSHIRE

With such a diverse range of produce; from beer to chocolate, baked goods to home-reared fruit and veg. There's never been a better reason to buy locally.

Made in Derbyshire is a celebration of the many places, people and producers of Derbyshire who make the county such a vibrant place to live and work.

Derbyshire is at the centre of England and has a rich food and drink heritage that is still very much alive today.

The Bakewell Pudding is world renowned, mineral water from Ashbourne and Buxton are household brands, and Hartington in Derbyshire is where Stilton cheese is made. Derbyshire is also home to many micro-breweries, such as the award winning Roman inspired Derventio Brewery and the traditional "born in a barn" Peak Ales. Across the county you'll also find delectable chocolatiers such as Holdsworth Chocolates in Bakewell, creating exquisite handmade treats, and the unique sustainably sourced Chocolate by Design in Chesterfield. In addition, there's a plentiful supply of artisanal bakeries, such as Derby's Baked café, who make handmade cakes and delicious home cooked food to go alongside speciality teas and coffee. You'll also find places such as The Loaf in Crich, serving up café food and deli-style groceries, as well as delicious freshly baked cakes and breads. Businesses like these produce in partnership with the many farms across the region, giving us home-reared meats, fruit, vegetable and dairy products.

The Made in Derbyshire initiative also supports other kinds of businesses, from dance academies to independent furniture and fashion retailers as well as creative arts shops, schools and museums.

With stunning natural landscapes, historic towns and a growing city brimming with inspirational shops, places to eat and drink as well as producers of some of the most delicious food and drink in the country, there is plenty to explore in Derbyshire's culinary world.

If you would like to find out more about the businesses involved, and how you can help celebrate Derbyshire, then have a browse of the website **www.madeinderbyshire.org**.

# A festival on THE MOVE

19-21st June 2015 marks the return of the 'most handsome festival in the world' as Eroica Britannia set up their three-day festival camp in Bakewell.

The inaugural Eroica Britannia – a three-day vintage cycling and lifestyle festival – swept into Derbyshire in June 2014.

Inspired by the original Italian L'Eroica ('the heroes') ride – dubbed 'the most handsome festival in the world' – it features pre-1987 bikes ridden by 3,500 adventurers in glorious period costume.

The Eroica Britannia ride is famed for its gruelling Peak District routes, but it also celebrates the best of British – including food and drink. The ride begins and ends at Bakewell Showground, which is crammed full of award-winning vendors in the Graze food festival area.

Graze is designed to enhance the festival with an eclectic mix of award-winning food, from street traders to purveyors of the best tastes in the land. Individual outlets create a 'theatre' of cuisine, enabling diners to sample food from every continent.

Festival-goers wandering along the rows of food stalls will discover French Crêpiers trained in Brittany rubbing shoulders with master coffee baristas; spicy Malay food is served up next to sizzling Mexican delights. Street food is the watchword – from the best flavour-packed paella from Seville to huge pans of rich French cassoulet or baskets of chicken and chips.

The food is global, but with a commitment from all of Graze's traders to source the finest local produce. From breakfast through to supper, there is a variety of tempting treats for cyclists and spectators alike – not forgetting the special Eroica beer brewed by Bakewell's Thornbridge Brewery.

Eroica Britannia has short, medium and long routes depending on riders' ability. They take in the iconic Monsal, Tissington and High Peak trails and call at six Peak villages, which also host their own mini festivals for riders to enjoy local food and drink along the route.

Photo courtesy of: Polly A Baldwin Dynamic Pictures

The event has been named as one of the best value family festivals in the UK by Visit England. It additionally features live music, entertainment, acres of vintage stalls and experiences.

Vintage is vogue at Eroica Britannia, as exemplified by the Best in Show fancy dress competition – judges include Patrick Grant from the Great British Sewing Bee and there are top prizes to be won from the iconic Liberty, London.

There's even help to get ready in the British Bazaar; barbers and hair salons offer wet shaves and make-up while kit and clothing outlets are perfect for lifestyle requirements.

The family sports day has a vintage twist too; think egg and spoon, three-legged races, tug-of-war and sack races – there's fun for mums and dads as well as the kids.

Shoppers are not forgotten – there are hardware and cook shops, florists, antique furniture and homeware, bookshops, magazine stands and more in an area inspired by bygone eras, wanderlust, sustainability and provenance.

When it's time to kick back after a stroll or cycle, Hullabaloo is the festival's live entertainment area. Music, bands, theatre and other live entertainment has a vintage edge combined with modern elements, ensuring something for everyone. Those with energy left can even slip on their dancing shoes.

Weekend passes for 3 days are priced at £10 and under 12s go free. To find out more visit eroicabritannia.co.uk.

Photo courtesy of: James Brown 93ft

Photo courtesy of: Polly A Baldwin Dynamic Pictures

Photo courtesy of: James Brown 93ft

# There's much more TO DERBY

Derby has seen an impressive boom in recent years with the growth of both independents and chains leading the way.

Derby's food and drink scene has become increasingly diverse in recent years, thanks in part to a surge of independent eateries opening their doors during the recession.

A number of chains initially bypassed the city, giving entrepreneurs the perfect platform to launch something new – ideas formed in the heart of Derby by its locals, not by external corporations. One unique example is The Pyclet Parlour – a bakery and café in Derby's glorious Victorian Market Hall which serves traditional Derby Pyclets – the only establishment in the world to do so!

Success breeds success and, with these new outlets not just surviving but thriving, more and more cafés, bars and restaurants began popping up around the city.

Derby City Council's tourism team and Marketing Derby have been stalwart supporters of the city's increasingly cosmopolitan food scene, investing time and money to help the sector continue its growth and development, and to promote its diversity.

The Marketing Derby team has recognised the difficulties traders face and has worked to support and arm them with marketing tools, as well as instigating the Derby Food & Drink Awards in 2009.

The awards have proved hugely popular and were founded after whispers of complaint from consumers about having nowhere good to eat or drink in the city. The awards hold gravitas among diners and the recognition they bring for bars and eateries instils trust among consumers.

In addition, Marketing Derby has developed an online database of quality food and drink outlets on its website, which is kept updated by a specialist team with its finger on the foodie pulse. In an effort to keep information as up-to-date as possible, a complementing Taste Derby app has been developed, which iPhone and Android users can download to their smartphones.

Photo courtesy of: VisitEngland/Diana Jarvis

Photo courtesy of: Miles Dosher Photography

VisitEngland/Diana Jarvis

VisitEngland/Diana Jarvis

Photo courtesy of: Cactus Images

Photo courtesy of: Cactus Images

Photo courtesy of: VisitEngland/Diana Jarvis

Courtesy of: VisitEngland/Diana Jarvis

The app and website focus on restaurants bringing value and quality to Derby and users can browse by cuisine or type to find popular, unique establishments. Examples include the Little Chester Ale House, a converted former laundrette; Park Bikeworks, where premium bikes and coffee go hand-in-hand; and the soon-to-open Brooklyn Social, a casual diner fusing US 'dive bars' and East London watering holes in the city's bustling Cathedral Quarter.

Derby's real ale boom cannot be ignored either. The city hosts events including the National Winter Ales Festival and has been cited as the real ale capital of Britain by the Lonely Planet Guide, thanks to its abundance of craft breweries and the diversity of beers available in its pubs and bars.

The Guide's surveyors found over 170 different beers on sale in venues around the city in 2012, with a handful of pubs boasting ten or more real ales on tap, including The Flowerpot and The Five Lamps.

This success has been a contributing factor to Derby's food scene; many of the city's real ale pubs also serve good, hearty food in a considered, relaxed atmosphere appealing to a mature audience.

Unsurprisingly, these developments haven't gone unnoticed by national chains. The Intu shopping centre is now home to brands including Wagamama, Pizza Express and Nando's, with the addition of the trendy Byron Burger.

The bar for quality has been raised in Derby and the wealth of diversity among food and drink outlets now provides a host of opportunities for the public to experience something new and different. Marketing Derby has successfully helped to raise the profile of food and drink both in the city and further afield – and to challenge consumers' tastes and perceptions.

Photo courtesy of: VisitEngland/Diana Jarvis

Photo courtesy of: Matthew Jones

Rum BUTTER
Rum BUTTER
Brandy BUTTER
Nettle JELLY
Nettle JELLY

Rum BUTTER
Rum BUTTER
Brandy BUTTER
Nettle JELLY
Nettle JELLY

Photo courtesy of: VisitEngland/Diana Jarvis

AIRY FRESH

Photo courtesy of: VisitEngland/Diana Jarvis

Photo courtesy of: VisitEngland/Diana Jarvis

# Best In SHOW

The Bakewell Show show reflects farming and agriculture in our region. The food and farming tent is now one of the most popular attractions.

Food and the link between the plough and the plate has always been an important element of the Bakewell Show. But this came into sharp focus 26 years ago with the launch of British Food and Farming year.

A special committee has driven the initiative ever since giving specialist food producers a platform to display their goods and share their food philosophies.

The Food and Farming marquee is now one of the most popular sections of the historic show, which always takes place on the first Wednesday and Thursday in August.

The makeshift demonstration area of the early years evolved into a full-grown kitchen with high profile demonstrators including James Martin. More recently there have been other demonstrations of bread and cheese making as well as meat cutting.

The cheese competition, which had humble beginnings, has since become one of the most keenly-contested in the industry. Now housed in an air-conditioned tent, there are specialist entries such as chocolate and Christmas cake flavoured cheeses and traditional favourites such as Stilton and Cheddar. There is a cheese wedding cake challenge and

a celebration cheeseboard class. Meat products have been introduced too.

The importance of engaging children has never been underestimated. A dedicated children's section offers a variety of activities to demonstrate the food and farming link, and a special class was introduced in 2014 where two local children, guided by experts, got the chance to pick their favourite cheese. At one time a children's cheese sculpture competition was introduced and one year there was a mechanical cow for demonstrating milk production.

Even the Duchess of Devonshire got a chance to judge – selecting her Chatsworth Choice.

Reflecting changing tastes, the section has moved away from specifically British produce – and while acknowledging that British is best it encourages other food too – so now traditional pork butchers and pie makers sit comfortably alongside producers of specialist olives and continental cheeses.

Photo courtesy of: Steve Caddy

# Des Coleman's
# BULL'S HEAD LASAGNE

Derby local Des Coleman is known to many for his role as Lenny Wallace in EastEnders and as BBC East Midlands' flamboyant weatherman.

He originally trained as a fabricator welder, but it wasn't until a brush with the law – and a cathartic night discussing the future with two fellow inmates – that his career path changed.

Des followed his dream to entertain and enrolled in drama school. He flourished among like-minded, creative people and walked straight into a role in the West End musical Miss Saigon before hitting the big-time among Walford's best. Now, he presents on the Politics Show, performs as Sammy Davis Jr in the Rat Pack and is in the process of setting up the Des Coleman Performance Academy.

But, while career success was Des' for the taking, the same cannot be said for his foibles in the kitchen.

"My brothers and sisters all took an active interest in cooking," says Des. "But I saw it as time-consuming. Why would I want to watch a pan of rice boil? Think of all the other exciting things I could be doing in those 15 minutes! It's become a bit of a family joke..."

After kitchen calamities including attempting to cook meat from frozen by boiling it in water for an hour, Des has sensibly decided to leave things to the professionals.

The Bull's Head in the village of Monyash is a favourite dining spot for Des. After a Peak District walk with his family and friends, their lasagne is the best he's found since he first tried it in France many years ago. Serves 8.

## Ingredients

12 pasta sheets

**For the bolognese sauce:**

Vegetable oil

500g onions, finely chopped

3 cloves garlic, crushed

1400g mince

6g basil

6g oregano

240g tomato purée

500g chopped tomatoes

300g sliced mushrooms

125ml beef stock

100ml red wine

Salt and pepper

**For the cheese sauce:**

150g butter

150g flour

3½ pints milk

100g cheese

## Method

Place a pan on the hob and pour in a splash of oil to cover the base.

Add the onions and garlic and fry them off until soft. Then add the mince and cook until brown.

Stir in the tomato purée and mix well before adding the basil, oregano and seasoning.

Add the chopped tomatoes, red wine, beef stock and sliced mushrooms and bring to the boil, stirring occasionally. Simmer for 20-25 minutes.

Meanwhile, make the cheese sauce in a good heavy bottomed pan.

Melt the butter over a gentle heat. Add the flour and beat in well. Cook for a couple of minutes then season with salt and pepper to taste.

Gently add the milk, whisking all the time – it can help to warm the milk a little in the microwave to speed this process up!

When it comes to the boil beat in the grated cheese and mix until completely combined. The sauce should be of a good coating consistency.

Now layer up your lasagne; cover the base of your dish with a single layer of pasta, then a layer of bolognese and finally a swirl of cheese sauce across the meat. Next another layer of the same, finished with a layer of pasta. Top generously with cheese sauce.

Bake in oven 180°c for 20-30 minutes or until golden and bubbling.

Serve and enjoy.

# Chic and UNIQUE

'Anoki' is the Urdu word for 'unique' – and it's definitely that. A host of top awards and accolades has cemented its place in the region's culinary scene.

Restaurateur Naveed Khaliq's dream of creating a unique Indian dining experience was realised in 2003 with the launch of Anoki on Derby's London Road.

Anoki is the urdu word for 'unique' – the underlying ethos that runs through the whole Anoki experience.

The extensive refurbishment of what was once a dilapidated picture hall has resulted in a sumptuous and opulent dining hall.

Modern chandeliers suspend from its striking arched ceiling; one of the many architectural features which were carefully restored and enhanced.

The restaurant's authentic menu, developed with the help of Nav's parents, offers an insight into traditional Indian cuisine. Food is immaculately presented – as are the staff, who all wear traditional Indian dress.

The varied menu is created using the finest ingredients and features dishes such as lamb haandi, which uses choice cuts of lamb cooked slowly on the bone, tandoori sea bass and desi lamb, a village dish from North India.

There are also 'feature dishes' – specialities and unique culinary creations from Anoki's team of chefs – and favourites including chicken tikka, tandoori vegetables and balti special mix.

Since opening, Anoki Derby has collected a host of accolades including Retail Business of the Year at the inaugural Derby Telegraph Awards and the Excellence in Customer Service award at the Derbyshire Chamber Awards 2014.

It has also been recognised on a national level in the Michelin Guide, in the Sunday Times' Top 10 Places to Eat and was named Best Indian restaurant in the Midlands in the Cobra Good Curry Guide the same year.

Anoki also boasts a private dining room and a function and events suite where bespoke menus can be enjoyed to suit any occasion. Sunday is a special banquet evening and Monday is barbecue night, featuring a selection of dishes from the Anoki tandoor.

Anoki

# Anoki
# LAHOORI GOSHT

The central tenets to a great curry are trial and error, confidence and an enjoyment of cooking. A well-used cliché by many cooks, but with good grounds!

In terms of quantities, of spices in particular, they are just a guide – and can be varied according to individual tastes and preference.

A lot of the ingredients listed are optional (marked as such). They add to the flavour, but the recipe works just as well without (the optional spices are not always easily available).

If you are cooking for two people, I'd recommend freezing half after cooking.

Serves 4.

## Ingredients

Cooking oil

1kg lamb (off the bone) cut into bite size pieces

2 small onions, peeled and sliced

4 ripe tomatoes, chopped into small chunks

4 cloves garlic, chopped or crushed

Small piece of ginger, chopped or crushed

Salt, to taste

Chilli powder, to taste (½ tsp or more, depending on how hot you want it)

½ tsp turmeric powder

½ tsp coriander powder

Fresh coriander, chopped

½ tsp jeera powder (optional)

2 green chillies, chopped (optional)

2 whole small green cardamons (optional)

3 whole cloves (optional)

1 cinnamon stick (optional)

4 whole black peppercorns (optional)

## Method

Heat the oil in a wok or pan, add all the whole spices and fry for 20 seconds.

Add the onions, ginger and garlic.

Fry on a low heat for one minute.

Add the lamb and stir for 30 seconds.

Add ½ cup of water.

Cover and leave for 30 minutes on a medium heat. Check every 10 minutes and stir. Add water if it starts to evaporate.

Depending on the quality of lamb, in approximately 30 minutes it should be tender, (at this point the water should have all but dried out).

Turn the heat to full and add the powder spices – turmeric, chilli powder, coriander powder, jeera powder and green chillies (dependent on how hot you like it).

Stir for 30 seconds.

Add chopped tomatoes and stir for 2-3 minutes. The lamb should be really tender by now (if not add more water and cover again on a low flame until tender).

Add the fresh coriander and serve.

*Tip: Spices only cook in oil, so ensure oil is visible on the surface before adding the powdered spices, if not turn the heat to full until some water evaporates.*

# _Traditional_ PERFECTION

With baking knowledge handed down from her Nan, Lucy Cassar's Apple Tree embraces traditional recipes and values with modern flair.

The Apple Tree Gift Shop & Teahouse in the village of Ockbrook has become a community hub since opening in March 2012 – it even attracted the attention of chef extraordinaire Heston Blumenthal.

Proprietor Lucy Cassar was approached to appear on the acclaimed chef's Great British Food programme in 2014 to try his creative take on afternoon tea as a thank you for keeping the tradition alive in her own establishment.

It's Lucy's commitment and passion for tradition that sets The Apple Tree apart. She strove to make her dream of owning a 'treasure trove' gift shop a reality, and sought creative ways to develop a warm, welcoming atmosphere to avoid the often clinical shop feel.

This, combined with a love of baking instilled by her Nan Joan Stafford, sparked the addition of the Apple Tree's 1950s vintage tea room. Drinks are served in good china, an array of cupcakes whisper enticingly to diners, and service is exemplary – The Apple Tree was a finalist in the Best Customer Service category at the Derby Food & Drink Awards in 2014.

Light lunches are also available and delectable cakes range from a classic Victoria sponge to salted caramel and lemon meringue bakes – Nan Joan, now 92-years-old, even contributes a cake on occasion! Coffee is freshly ground as required, quiche is homemade by the local butcher and, of course, the traditional afternoon and cream teas are a menu highlight.

The Apple Tree has become so popular that most lunchtimes are fully booked, but expansion of the tea room is planned to cope with customer demand.

Plenty of gifts and trinkets can be found in the shop: hand finished cards, books, jewellery, candles, scarves and other treasures line the shelves. Lucy works hard to source individual, high-end items from craftspeople, both locally and further afield, so customers can always be sure of finding a unique present.

The Apple Tree

Gift Shop and Teahouse

you need is love

# The Apple Tree

## LUCY'S LEMON, LIME & RASPBERRY MOJITO LOAF

Love a Mojito? We love turning cocktails into cakes – and this is our ultimate sunshine season cake that oozes summer flavours and fun. Once you've mastered the basics, you can easily adapt this recipe to any cocktail.
Serves 8-10.

## Ingredients

**For the cake:**

3 eggs

170g margarine

170g caster sugar

170g self-raising flour

1 tsp baking powder

Handful of frozen raspberries

1 lemon

1 lime

**For the drizzle:**

½ a lemon, juiced

1 tbsp caster sugar

1 tbsp white rum

**For the frosting:**

100g cream cheese

50g unsalted butter

250g icing sugar

3 tbsp white rum

1 lemon

1 lime

Stem of fresh mint

## Method

Preheat the oven to 170°c.

Combine the margarine and sugar and whisk until smooth and fluffy. Gently whisk in the eggs then fold in the self-raising flour and baking powder. Grate the lemon and lime zest and add it to the cake mixture.

Add the juice of one lime and crush a handful of frozen raspberries into the cake mixture then stir well. Pour the mixture into a greased and lined 2lb loaf tin.

Bake for 35-40 minutes or until a skewer can be inserted into the centre of the cake and it comes out clean.

Make your drizzle by combining the lemon juice, caster sugar and white rum.

Once out of the oven leave the cake to stand for 5 minutes then prick all over with a skewer. Drizzle the rum, sugar and lemon mixture over the top of the warm cake and leave to cool.

Finally make your cream cheese frosting. Whisk the butter, cream cheese, white rum and icing sugar in a bowl until you get a firm consistency.

If it's too runny add more icing sugar, or if it's too solid add more cream cheese (or rum!). When you're happy with the consistency spread the icing on the top of the loaf. We leave the icing to set before adding the finishing touches.

Cut the lemon and lime into wedges. Add these and a stem of fresh mint to the top of the cake to garnish.

Serve – reminding your friends it contains neat rum – and enjoy!

# The Apple Tree
## DOUBLE CHOCOLATE FUDGE BROWNIE

This is an extremely popular choice at The Apple Tree. "It's taken us three years of experimenting to perfect the recipe and it's incredibly rewarding when our customers can't believe this gooey brownie is gluten free." Serves 9.

## Ingredients

250g dark chocolate

250g butter

4 eggs

360g dark brown sugar

2 tsp vanilla bean extract

150g cocoa powder

50g gluten-free flour

1 tsp xanthan gum

100g white chocolate

1 tsp baking powder

A pinch of salt

## Method

Preheat oven to 170°c.

Bring an inch of water to a simmer in a pan. Place a heatproof bowl in the mouth of the pan and put in the dark chocolate, butter and a pinch of salt. Stir until melted and remove the bowl from the heat to allow the mixture to cool.

In the meantime whisk together the eggs, brown sugar and vanilla bean extract then add the cooled chocolate mixture to the egg mixture.

Fold in the cocoa powder, flour, xanthan gum and baking powder.

Roughly chop the bar of white chocolate and add it to the mixture. Pour into a greased and lined 177mm square tin and bake for 40 minutes.

Remove the brownie and allow to cool. For maximum fudge texture place in the fridge overnight. When serving cut into nine squares with a warm, sharp knife. Dust with icing sugar et voilà!

*Tip: If you'd like to make this brownie, but you're not gluten intolerant, simply replace the gluten free flour and xanthan gum with 50g of self-raising flour.*

# Baked to PERFECTION

Self-taught bakers Victoria Bate and Garry Baker offer a huge variety of breads and popular sweets – all made from scratch and delicious to the last crumb.

Since opening in 2012, Baked artisan bakery and café has become a home from home for proprietors Victoria and Garry.

The day begins early for them when they get up to bake the bread and cakes. They then open the doors to the contemporary coffee shop, located on The Strand in Derby's historic cathedral quarter. Victoria works front of house during the day, ensuring customers are always greeted by a friendly face.

It's this level of personal service that makes Baked's many regulars feel as though they are welcomed into Victoria and Garry's own living room. There is a warm homely feel to the café. Victoria knows most of their regulars by name and many have become friends, not only to Victoria and Garry but of each other. So much so that there is a trip to Whitby planned for summer.

Victoria taught herself and Garry to bake bread and they have honed their skills, now baking a wide selection of artisan breads including the popular chorizo, chilli and cheese loaf, rye breads and spelt for those with gluten and wheat intolerances.

There is a strong emphasis on quality local produce at Baked and like the bread everything is made from scratch. This includes popular sweet treats such as Bakewell cake, lemon drizzle and Garry's mum Gabrilelle's Eccles cakes. Polish apple cake and Polish breads are regular features on Saturdays, giving a nod to Victoria's heritage.

It's not only the food that is good at Baked, the café serves a wide range of excellent teas and coffees, all made to the same high standard customers have come to expect.

Their efforts speak for themselves but if that isn't enough, then take into account Baked's award winning status; Best Newcomer in the Derby Food and Drink awards 2012, Best café finalist in 2013 and runners up in the Best Independent Retailer category at the Observer Food Monthly awards in 2014.

# *Baked Artisan's*
# ROASTED RED PEPPER SOUP

With granary bread. Serves 4-6.

## Ingredients

### For the soup:

3 tbsp rapeseed oil

1 medium onion, finely diced

2 medium carrots, finely diced

6 red peppers, quartered and seeds removed

½ can chopped tomatoes

1 litre vegetable stock

½ tsp dried chilli flakes

Sea salt and freshly ground black pepper

### For the granary loaf's sourdough starter:

300g strong white bread flour

Water

### For the granary loaf:

285g light malthouse flour

265g stoneground wholemeal flour

60g seeds

380ml water at room temperature

6g salt

6g fresh yeast

100g sourdough starter

## Method

### For the soup

Preheat the oven to 220°c (200°c fan).

Toss the peppers in a tablespoon of the rapeseed oil and spread out on a baking tray. Roast for 25-30 minutes.

Set aside and leave to cool; remove skins and roughly chop.

Sauté the onion and carrots in the remaining oil for 10-15 minutes or until the onions are translucent and the carrots are soft.

Add the chilli flakes and cook for 1 minute.

Add the chopped tomatoes, peppers and ¾ of the vegetable stock. Bring to the boil and simmer for 15 minutes.

Remove from the heat and blend until smooth. Add the remaining stock if required for the desired consistency. Season to taste with salt and pepper

### For the starter

#### Day 1

Mix 50ml room temperature water with 60g of the flour in a large kilner jar. Leave covered at room temperature for 24 hours.

#### Day 2

Feed the sourdough with another 50ml room temperature water and the remaining flour. Mix well, cover and leave for 24 hours.

On days 3, 4 and 5 repeat day 2.

By day 6 the sourdough starter should be bubbly and active, meaning it is ready to use.

### For the granary loaf

Preheat oven to its highest setting.

Mix the sourdough starter with the water and add the flours and seeds followed by the yeast and salt.

Mix thoroughly to combine, then knead the dough for 10-15 minutes until smooth and elastic.

Place the dough in an oiled bowl. Cover with a clean, dry tea towel and leave in a warm room or airing cupboard for 1 hour or until doubled in size.

Remove the dough from the bowl, knock it back and divide into two.

Shape each ball of dough into a dome and place on a baking tray. Put back in a warm place for 40 minutes or until doubled in size.

When the dough is ready, put the tray straight into the oven and reduce the temperature to 210°c. Bake for 15 minutes, then reduce the temperature to 160°c and bake for a further 15 minutes.

Remove from the oven and leave to cool on a rack before serving.

# The traditional METHOD

Using artisinal baking techniques handed down by master bakers, the Bakewell Bakery produces some of the finest loaves we've ever tasted.

The Bakewell Bakery was founded in 2011 out of owners Nick and Jemma Beagrie's belief in traditional artisan methods. They were moving production to create more space for customers, when they stumbled upon the perfect bakery location in Bakewell's Riverside Business Park.

Keen to uphold tradition, the Beagries' set about employing skilled bakers to create products by hand. The bakery operates without the use of plant machinery, which helps to maintain exceptional quality and protect the dying art of craft baking.

Finding such a high level of skill has been no mean feat – one specialist baker even travels daily from his home in Lancashire to work in The Bakewell Bakery. Nick and Jemma have invested in training people from scratch, making the enterprise an excellent option for bakers aspiring to learn classic methods.

Even their Bakewell pudding maker (who was trained by the Old Bakewell Pudding Shop's previous master baker) now has over 20 years of service under his belt.

It is not surprising, then, that the bakery's products are an instant hit. The business has flourished and become a 24-hour operation; bread is baked through the night using only English flour, while puddings and cakes made using local eggs are created during the day.

There are around 50 varieties of bread to choose from, including black treacle loaf and brioche buns, while fresh lemon cake, tray bakes and, of course Bakewell Puddings, are best sellers.

Delivery is available six days a week and the bakery supplies both private customers and hospitality outlets such as cafés, farm shops, restaurants and hotels in Derbyshire and South Yorkshire.

# Bakewell Bakery
## BLACK TREACLE COB

Makes 2 loaves.

## Ingredients

500g granary flour

60g salt

16g yeast

320ml warm water

100g black treacle

5g sesame seeds

5g poppy seeds

5g oats

5g sunflower seeds

1 medium egg

Ice cubes

## Method

Mix the flour and salt together and add in the yeast and black treacle. Stir in the water until you have a smooth dough.

Knead by hand for 5-10 minutes.

Put the dough back in the bowl and prove in a warm place for 30 minutes.

Knock back the dough then knead for a few more minutes.

Separate the dough in two and mould into bloomer shapes. Alternatively you could add the dough mixture to two 400g loaf tins.

Brush the top of the bloomers or loaves with egg wash and sprinkle the dough with the mixture of sesame, poppy and sunflower seeds and oats.

Set aside for 60-90 minutes or until the dough has doubled in size.

Bake for 25 minutes at 215°c.

To make the bread crusty, add ice cubes in a ramekin dish to the bottom of the oven.

# Straight to THE POINT

Good tools in the kitchen are essential – we speak to the experts at the Bakewell Cookshop.

Bakewell Cookshop is an Aladdin's cave of glimmering knives, kitchen gadgets, gifts and homeware. Any budding chef or baker could spend hours perusing the shelves of innovative, covetable items, from artisan ceramics to futuristic garlic presses and a stunning array of knives.

The business was originally established as an online outlet in 2012 by Mark Pilkington and David Kidd, both industry experts who had previously designed and produced knives and other kitchen equipment for a number of worldwide brands and retailers.

The website proved so popular that they decided to establish a small shop in Bakewell the following year. Popularity led to yet further expansion and the shop moved once again to its current home on Matlock Street – while still retaining a popular sales outlet via the website.

Knives are a speciality here. It's where Mark and David's passion and expertise lies, having helped design many of the items and packaging stocked in their shop today. They still work heavily on design in their studio above the shop creating products for Sheffield knife makers and retailers including John Lewis and Lakeland.

They have also started their own range, Nosh, which comprises a selection of beautifully finished wooden chopping and serving boards and cheese knife sets. Nosh is now stocked by other UK retailers too and there are plans to expand the range following the success of the brand in Australia, Holland and more recently in Japan.

Mark and David's enthusiasm has been embraced by relatives and the business has become very much a family affair. Mark's son Joe is shop manager and website guru, while wife Sally and their nephew Sam Cox also work in the business and David's mum Catherine lends a hand with social media.

The family vibe makes for a warm, friendly welcome and, whether you're an expert cook, or enjoy baking as a hobby, Bakewell Cookshop is a great place to pick up equipment you just can't be without.

# Bakewell Cookshop
## SHEFFIELD KNIFE RECIPE

A good knife is made from the right ingredients, baked at the optimum temperature, for the perfect amount of time with extra skill and knowledge added for a professional finish.

## Ingredients

**For good quality blade steel, take iron and add:**

*A pinch of carbon
to increase hardness*

*A dash of chromium
for corrosion resistance*

*A splash of vanadium and
molybdenum to improve the
hardening process*

## Method

Place in oven at 1110°c for approximately two hours (times and temperatures vary depending on oven).

Carefully heat your ingredients to the right temperature for correct hardness. Too high and you risk making the knife blade too brittle, too low and the knife becomes soft and will not retain an edge.

Leave to cool.

Grind the blade at an angle of 20° each side. Attach preferred handle. Finally, whet the edge of the blade to achieve the characteristic razor sharp edge of a Sheffield-made knife.

Store in a knife block or use a blade guard to protect the edge; sharpen regularly. Wash with warm, soapy water and dry immediately, avoid using a dishwasher regardless of what the packaging may say.

Only use on wooden or plastic chopping boards to avoid dulling the edge.

Follow this advice and your knives will last a lifetime.

### Knife tips

Sharp knives are much safer than blunt knives. Less force is needed to slice or chop, which means you're less likely to slip. All knives need sharpening regardless of the quality.

The 'tomato test' is a good way of telling whether or not you need to hone or sharpen your knives: if your knife cannot cut through a tomato without squashing, it's time to sharpen or hone it. We recommend a good two-stage knife sharpener, which can do both.

Old, neglected knives should be replaced. A loose handle is an accident waiting to happen; rust on a blade will transfer to food and corrosion will cause a blade to weaken.

# *Roll out* THE BARREL

The panarama from the Barrel Inn is simply breathtaking with views over five counties – though it is the highest pub in Derbyshire.

Diane and Phil Cone are oracles of the pub world having run establishments in Derbyshire for over 30 years.

Following stints at the Plough in Hathersage and the Sir William in Grindleford, they now preside over The Barrel Inn at Bretton, where they have been since 1996. They were joined by son Tom in 2011, further developing the pub's warm family feel.

The Barrel would be at the top of any publican's wish list; it is the highest pub in Derbyshire and the panoramic countryside views are simply spectacular – on a clear day it is possible to see five counties.

The view has been enjoyed by customers since 1597 when the inn was built on the old turnpike road from Sheffield to Manchester, via Buxton.

Its location and four ensuite bedrooms make The Barrel as popular today as ever. It is an ideal base for walkers and those wishing to explore the area's historic villages.

Food has been carefully considered. As much as possible is made in-house using produce from local suppliers, including The Herb Table, Waterall's Pork Butchers and Hancock's Butchers at Castlegate Farm, whose animals can be seen grazing from the pub on a clear day.

Menus are a team effort with the staff contributing ideas to head chef Matthew Ball, who has worked with the Cones for over 20 years. The fare is traditional, hearty and varied; alongside the core menu are regularly changing specials such as venison, lamb and vegetarian options, plus a tempting dessert menu.

Pies and pasties are popular and made fresh to order. The Bretton Pasty has been specially created using lamb shoulder, which Diane slow-roasts in the Aga overnight. It is served with mushy peas, chips and gravy – a favourite for regulars.

Enjoy all this with a glass of wine or a real ale by the roaring log fire in the winter, or outside on the terrace in the summer.

The Barrel Inn

# The Barrel Inn
## BRETTON PASTY

Serves 4.

## Ingredients

**For the pastry:**

450g plain flour

225g butter

2 eggs, lightly beaten

Pinch of salt

Water (a few drops to form the pastry)

1 egg for egg wash

**For the filling:**

1 medium shoulder of lamb on the bone

1 large onion

1 medium swede

3 large carrots

2-3 celery sticks

1 dessert spoon mint sauce

2-3 sprigs rosemary

2-3 sprigs thyme

2-3 cloves garlic

Knob of butter

Few drops of vegetable oil

Salt and pepper

## Method

### For the pastry

Put the flour in the bowl with a pinch of salt. Rub in the butter until the mixture looks like breadcrumbs.

Make a well in the centre and add the eggs. Bring the mixture together then knead to form a dough. Place in the fridge to chill for 30 minutes.

### For the filling

Place the shoulder of lamb in a roasting tin and make small incisions in the skin with a knife. Peel and slice the garlic cloves and push them into the incisions with sprigs of rosemary. Cover with parchment and foil, sealing round the edges.

The meat needs to be cooked on a low heat for several hours. We suggest initially cooking at a high heat for 30 minutes before turning the oven down to approximately 135°c and cooking until the meat is coming away from the bone – we slow-roast ours overnight in the Aga.

Once cooked and cool enough to handle, strip the meat from the bone and cut into small pieces. Strain the juices through a sieve and reserve the liquor.

Wash, peel and dice the vegetables to roughly 1.5cm and remove the thyme from the stalks. Add to a thick-bottomed pan and sweat everything off in a little butter and oil until softened.

Add the lamb meat and juices to the vegetables and bring to a simmer. Stir in the mint sauce and season with salt and pepper, then leave to cool.

To make the pasties, roll out the pastry and cut out circles – you could use a side plate for a template.

Place a good amount of the cooled filling into the centre of each circle. Brush round the edges with water or beaten egg and pinch together with your fingers to make a pasty shape.

Brush with beaten egg and cook in the oven for roughly 20 minutes at 180°c.

*Tip: You might have to make additional pastry to use up any leftover filling – or of course you can freeze the filling for use at a later date.*

# All day and all of THE NIGHT

Building on the success of their daytime eatery, Bean Caffé now extend into the night when they transform into the trendy 'Hide' Burger Bar.

Mother and daughter partnership Sarah and Liv Pritchard have stormed to success with their Bean Caffé brand, making their outlets some of the most popular in Derby.

Their first site opened in the city's Friargate Studios in 2010 after Sarah spotted the potential for a new concept. Installing Mac computers and fast internet made the urban space an immediate hit with the business community and word soon spread.

The outlet won Best Café in the Derby Food & Drink Awards in 2012 and 2014 and was commended for its range of food. Breakfasts include Eggs Barcelona – scrambled egg on a toasted bagel with chilli, tomatoes and chorizo – and innovative Oatmeal Latte Porridge.

Lunch options include salads, stews and the popular 'sophisticated macaroni cheese', complemented by a specials board and homemade cakes. The coffee is from Sheffield-based ethical company Café Cereza.

Sarah also attributes success to Bean's 'fantastic foodie, perfectionist chefs' and front-of-house teams, whose attention to detail and welcoming smiles have helped shape the café's personality.

Sarah and Liv's quest for new things led to the opening of their second Bean Caffé in November 2014 at Riverside Chambers, the former magistrates' court – but with a Jekyll and Hyde twist.

By day the café operates in the same way as its namesake but with a slightly different feel – the old courtroom benches provide seating, the service counter is made from the dock and prisoners' cell keys adorn the walls.

By night it transforms into Hide, a candlelit burger bar with a relaxed, feel-good vibe. The idea came after barbecuing their homemade burgers at food festivals, weddings and private parties – which always went down a treat.

The organic burgers are 100% meat, which comes from Limousin-Angus cross cattle at Hill Farm, Bakewell, via butcher Rob Stafford in Mickleover. The simple but robust menu offers a variety of quality burgers and sides. Bacon is also local and ketchup, mayonnaise and relishes are made in-house.

Food can be washed down with a selection of craft beers – and a soundtrack of music is recommended by customers.

# Bean Callé's
# SOPHISTICATED MACARONI CHEESE

With cured ham, smoked paprika and Colston Basset Stilton. Serves 6.
Take these simple, easily sourced, local ingredients to create a good, honest
meal to share with friends and family.

## Ingredients

500g small cut macaroni (fresh is best, but dried is just as good!)

2-3 tbsp olive oil

1 red onion, finely chopped

1 chilli

1 large red pepper, thinly sliced

3 heaped tsp sweet smoked paprika

150g dried cured ham

1 clove garlic, grated

400g tinned cherry tomatoes

1 bottle of your favourite red wine (60ml required for cooking)

400ml double cream

200g mature cheddar

150g Stilton

60g grated Parmesan

50g fresh breadcrumbs

Freshly ground black pepper

1 pinch Maldon sea salt

## Method

Cook the macaroni until slightly under-cooked, then run under cold water in a colander to stop the cooking process. Drain and set aside to cool.

Next, grate the cheeses and mix together, saving 20g of Parmesan for the topping.

Now get your best blades ready for slicing and dicing! Finely slice the chilli and the red onion and cut the red pepper into thin strips. Roughly dice the dry cured ham.

Take the red wine and measure out 60ml and set aside… the rest of the bottle is for you, so pour a large glass and indulge!

Sauté the chillies and red onion in a large thick-bottomed pan over a medium heat for about 5 minutes, or until just starting to colour.

Add the paprika, ham and garlic and cook gently for another minute.

To this add the red wine and tomatoes and simmer gently for 20-30 minutes until the mixture has reduced and appears thick and glossy.

Add the Maldon sea salt and a good twist of black pepper.

Pour the cream into a thick-bottomed pan and heat until just simmering then whisk in the cheeses.

Place the pasta into a large bowl, add the cured ham mixture and the warm cream sauce. Adjust the seasoning to your liking.

Mix the breadcrumbs with the remaining Parmesan. If you like add a few fresh herbs such as basil or chives.

Grab your gratin dish and pour the macaroni mixture in. Sprinkle the breadcrumb mixture on top and place under a preheated grill for 5-10 minutes until bubbling and golden.

Serve immediately with a big bowl of dressed salad and the rest of your wine.

# Hide Burger Bar's
# CHILLI & CHORIZO RELISH

This relish is used in Hide's popular chilli burger along with sweet fiery peppers, crispy onions and signature homemade pickles and sauces. It needs to be mothered – before it's smothered! Serves 6.

## Ingredients

150g chorizo, finely diced

5 red chillies (leave the spicy seeds in for a hotter relish)

200g red onion, finely diced

Concasse of 5 vine ripened or Heritage tomatoes (skinned, deseeded and roughly chopped)

3 heaped tbsp soft brown sugar

75ml red wine vinegar

## Method

Place a heavy-bottomed pan on a low heat.

Into the dry pan add the finely diced chorizo. Gently sauté until the natural oils are released from the sausage.

Add the red onion and chillies then sauté until translucent.

Next add the tomatoes and stir in, followed by the brown sugar and red wine vinegar.

Stir until all the ingredients are fully combined – now the mothering comes in. Stay by the stove whilst you gently stir for 15-20 minutes until it appears sticky, with a jam-like consistency.

Adjust the seasoning to your taste – you may need to add a little more sugar if it is too tart for your taste buds.

*Tip: This is a tasty relish that can be used to enhance many foods – you don't just have to save it for your burgers.*

Add some to a doorstep mature cheddar sandwich filled with watercress to make it sparky!

Or toast a muffin, butter it and top with lightly poached eggs and a dollop of relish to brighten your morning.

Even a bowl of macaroni cheese comes to life with a heaped spoonful on top.

# Sunshine GOODNESS

With many health benefits, and a high cooking temperature, rapeseed oil is perfect for the kitchen.

England's sunny yellow rapeseed fields are a striking sight when in flower – but for Kate Brocklehurst it's not just about the aesthetics.

Kate joined forces with her partner Ben Furness – both foodies from Derbyshire farming families – after they were inspired to extract oil from the Brocklehurst family's rapeseed fields.

Kate's father Neil, who predominantly farms beef, had always grown rapeseed as a break crop for soil nutrition at the family farm in Ashford-in-the-Water. Between the three of them, Brock & Morten was born in 2013 – derived from the family surname and Kate's mum's maiden name.

Rapeseed's popularity has been on the increase in recent years, although Brock & Morten's is far from the mass produced bottles found in supermarkets.

Theirs is cold pressed; the seed is squeezed at a low temperature to extract the oil so the natural nutrients are preserved. Once settled, the oil is filtered and bottled, eliminating any need for heating or chemicals.

The Brocklehursts, including Kate's brother William, also bale the stems into straw for cattle bedding, and the shells are pressed into pellets which are fed back to their cows, ensuring no part of the rapeseed is wasted.

Rapeseed oil is mild with an earthy, creamy flavour, and has a higher burn point than many other oils – making it a perfect choice for cooking. It is also ideal for drizzling and salad dressings, which has led Brock & Morten to branch into flavoured oils including garlic, chilli, lemon and basil.

There are notable health benefits too, with the oil having half the saturated fat of olive oil and ten times more Omega 3.

Brock & Morten oil is used by a number of Derbyshire restaurants, including Fischer's at Baslow Hall and The Packhorse at Little Longstone (recipe page 141). It can be bought at local farm shops, including Chatsworth (recipe page 67), as well as farmers' markets across the county.

# The BAR EXAM

Situated in the old courthouse, the Buxton Tap House offers
a phenomenal range of draft and bottled beers from around the globe.

The Buxton Tap House lies within the High Peak town's buzzing café quarter on George Street, just a stone's throw from the iconic Opera House and Grade I listed Buxton Crescent.

Created in an extension of the town's former courthouse, the bar contains various nods to its history; antique windows have been unblocked and restored, while a vintage wall safe now houses flickering candles. This all combines seamlessly with Tap House's sleek, modern restoration, which was completed in 2013.

Run by Buxton Brewery, the pub is a showcase for the brewery's creations. There are 13 Buxton draft beers on tap at any one time and more than 80 different bottled beers from craft breweries around the globe. Wine features prominently too and is complemented by artisan gins, rums, vodkas and whiskies.

Beer tasters are available, enabling drinkers to try before they buy and discover new styles in the process. The Tap House has even started hosting tutored tastings, where its knowledgable staff impart wisdom learned at 'beer school'. These are Buxton Brewery's training sessions, which include brewery tours and brew days for staff.

Food hasn't been an afterthought either. The kitchen is home to a smoker, which is regularly loaded up with beef ribs, pulled pork, fresh fish and chicken. The Tap House smokes these meats over mesquite, hickory, apple and pear woods; the chefs are also partial to throwing in remnants of Scotch and Bourbon barrels, which have been used to age beer in the brewery, for a unique flavour.

Vegetarian dishes and Sunday roasts are also available, offering varied dining options every day of the week.

Live music and open mic nights are gaining in popularity too, so whether it's excellent beer, delicious food or great entertainment you're after, the Buxton Tap House has it all under one roof.

# Buxton Tap House
## SMOKED BEEF BRISKET

Meltingly soft brisket is one of life's simple pleasures – and not many things are more pleasurable than tucking into this recipe. Serves 6-8.

## Ingredients

**For the rub:**

10g fennel seeds

1 tsp cumin seeds

1 tsp black peppercorns

1 tsp coriander seeds

100g soft brown sugar

50g granulated sugar

10g garlic powder

100g fine salt

15g smoked paprika

30g paprika

1 tsp dried oregano

1 tsp cayenne pepper

**For the brisket:**

2.5kg beef brisket

Garnishes of your choice

## Method

**For the rub**

Toast the fennel, coriander, cumin seeds and peppercorns in a dry pan over a medium heat for a few minutes, shaking the pan until the spices release an aroma. Tip into a bowl and leave to cool.

Blitz the toasted spices in a blender until it becomes a rough powder. Combine with the remaining ingredients and mix well. Keep in a sealed container for up to a week.

**For the brisket**

Generously apply the rub to the meat, ensuring it is covered.

Place the brisket into a hot smoker with a handful of smoking chips and cook for 2½ hours at 275°c. If you are not using a smoker you can start the brisket off in a normal oven at 200°c for 45 minutes before moving on to the next step.

Remove the brisket from the oven or smoker, wrap in foil and place on a baking tray.

Cook the brisket at 90°c for 12 hours. When cooked remove the meat from the foil and keep any cooking juices for the gravy.

To serve, take three decent size slices of the brisket and place in the centre of a wooden board on top of rocket and watercress. Serve with sauerkraut, mustard, pickles, slaw, gravy and bread.

# Seasonal VARIETY

A staggering variety of fresh seasonal produce is on offer at the Chatsworth Farm Shop as well as fresh bread and cakes baked daily.

Chatsworth Farm Shop is renowned throughout Derbyshire and beyond for its unrivalled local produce. Located on the Chatsworth estate, it has established itself as a true destination venue and attracts over one million visitors every year.

The shop was founded in 1977 by Deborah, Dowager Duchess of Devonshire, to make Chatsworth's produce available directly to people who wanted quality, locally grown food. It started off predominantly selling homegrown beef and lamb, but has since developed to offer a staggering variety of exclusive produce from local suppliers.

Led for over 30 years by manager Andre Birkett, the shop is also a fantastic outlet for start-ups and adheres to the ethos that good food begins with good suppliers. It has helped a number of traders to establish themselves.

Openness and ability to diversify has seen Chatsworth Farm Shop flourish into a one-stop outlet for quality food and drink.

The in-house bakery produces fresh bread and cakes seven days a week and the deli stocks a plethora of cooked meats, pies, pasties, pâtés and over 100 cheeses.

A diverse fish counter ensures that fishmongering skills aren't lost locally and the extensive pantry stocks cereals, preserves, beers, chocolates, fruits and vegetables.

Beef, lamb and venison are butchered on-site while pork, pheasants and other meat comes from local suppliers. There are 16 varieties of seasonal sausage available daily with around one tonne sold per week.

Additional produce – such as asparagus and rhubarb – is celebrated throughout the seasons and served alongside the shop in a café, which boasts spectacular countryside views.

The café serves delicious dishes created by expert chefs using as much farm shop produce as possible. The new patisserie counter is a highlight, serving temptations such as tart au citron and all manner of chocolate delights.

Any profits from the farm shop and café are driven directly back into the estate; funds go towards the upkeep of parkland and the fabric of Chatsworth House to ensure that it can be enjoyed for decades to come.

Chatsworth Farm Shop

POTATOES
ORIGIN-ENGLISH
60p PER KG

Heritage Carrots
Class 1
Origin: ENGLISH
£3·60 Kilo

Manx kippers
£9.95 per kg
Origin: Isle of Man   Net caught

Mackerel Fillet
£19.00 per kg
Origin: Scottish   Net caught

# Chatsworth Estate
# ROAST HAUNCH OF VENISON

With rosemary. Serves 6-8.

## Ingredients

1 boned and rolled haunch roast of venison (750g –1kg)

3 tbsp Brock & Morten rapeseed oil

1 lemon, juice and zest

2 tbsp fresh rosemary, chopped

20 small sprigs fresh rosemary

2 carrots, peeled and largely diced

2 parsnips, peeled and largely diced

2 large mild onions, peeled and sliced

2 potatoes, peeled and largely diced

300ml game or beef stock

Salt and freshly ground black pepper

## Method

Place the venison in a non-metallic dish. Pierce the meat in twelve places with a small sharp knife.

Mix the oil, lemon zest and juice, chopped rosemary, salt and pepper together and pour over the meat. Rub the marinade all over the haunch, cover and leave in a cool place to marinate for several hours or overnight.

Preheat the oven to 230°c. Insert 12 small sprigs of fresh rosemary into the slits. Weigh the venison and calculate the cooking time, allowing 15 minutes per 450g for medium venison and 20 minutes for well done.

Scatter the carrots, parsnips, potatoes, onions and the remaining sprigs of rosemary over the base of a very large roasting pan. Lift the venison out of the marinade and place on top of the vegetables. Pour over any remaining marinade.

Put into the oven for 15 minutes to seal and brown, then turn down the heat to 200°c and add the game or beef stock. Roast for the calculated time, basting frequently with the juices in the pan.

When the venison is cooked, transfer to a serving dish, cover loosely and allow to rest for 15 minutes in the cooled switched-off oven. This will make it easier to carve and re-distribute the juices throughout the venison. Transfer the vegetables to a serving dish and keep warm.

Carve the venison into generous slices and serve with the vegetables.

# Bourne to BE WILD

Denby Visitor Centre is a popular destination;
more so because of the fantastic Bourne Restaurant.

Denby Pottery has been creating its popular stoneware in the heart of Derbyshire since it was established in 1809. It has built a global reputation for producing consistently high quality products including plates, bowls and teapots, using mainly local clay.

Bourne's Restaurant serves afternoon tea to customers visiting the Pottery. With Denby's continued growth it has become a cornerstone of the outlet and local community, evolving into a family-friendly restaurant serving homemade, British-inspired food.

Bourne's is open daily from 9am to 5pm and the kitchen uses local produce where possible, sourced from the nearby greengrocer, butcher and baker.

Bacon and sausage cobs are choice breakfast fare, while lunch is a varied mix of sandwiches, toasties, panini's, jacket potatoes and salads. The core range is complemented by daily changing homemade specials, from homity pie, warm quiches and hot pots to seasonal soups such as autumnal pumpkin and spring vegetable.

A traditional carvery is a Sunday staple, and is so popular that it also runs on a selected weekday, while Friday's special is fish. Stopping in for 'Denby Blend' coffee and cake is top of many visitors' to-do list in order to enjoy cakes, biscuits, scones and more, baked freshly each morning. Festive treats such as hot cross buns, bonfire parkin and Christmas dinner can also be found on the menu throughout the year.

The restaurant has a choice of seating areas including the main restaurant, a roof terrace, outdoor picnic benches and the upstairs Danesby Room. Visitors can dine on rustic pine tables and chairs while food is served, of course, on beautiful Denby crockery.

Denby is also home to a Cookery Theatre, which plays host to events throughout the year including celebrity and guest chef demonstrations.

They also exhibit at food and drink fairs throughout the country – this gives them a chance to chat to their customers and also indulge in their love of great food.

Bourne's
RESTAURANT
Denby Visitor Centre

# Denby Pottery's
# IMPERIAL PUDDING

Serves 4.

## Ingredients

100g Madeira cake crumb or any preferred plain cake

1 orange, finely zested

100g caster sugar

400ml whole milk

45g unsalted butter

2 medium free range eggs at room temperature

8 tbsp strawberry and raspberry compote

Extra caster sugar for dusting

120g mixture of soft fruit

50g caster sugar

2 tbsp sweet wine or sherry

## Method

To make the compote mix together and slowly stew the soft fruit, 50g of caster sugar and sweet wine or sherry until just soft. Set aside to cool before using. Any remaining compote can be served as extra sauce.

Preheat the oven 170°c. Lightly butter four deep teacups and set them in a baking tray with an inch of water around.

In a bowl mix the cake crumbs, orange zest and 1 tablespoon of the sugar.

To make a custard warm the milk and butter in a pan until the butter has just melted, then pour over the cake crumbs. Stir well and leave to soak for 15 minutes. Then stir in lightly whipped egg yolks. Save the egg whites for later.

Pour the mixture into teacups. Bake for 15-20 minutes until just set and lightly brown around the edges. Remove from the oven and cool slightly before spooning the cold compote on top.

Whisk egg whites in a grease-free bowl until they form stiff peaks. Gradually whisk in the remaining sugar and continue to whisk until stiff and glossy. Spoon or pipe the mixture on top of the custards and compote, creating peaks. Sprinkle with a little caster sugar.

Return the custards to the oven and bake for about 10 minutes until the meringue is crisp and lightly golden. Serve warm or at room temperature with any remaining compote.

# Sam and Amy's
## MANLY FISHERMAN'S PIE

Sam Pinkham and Amy Voce are best known for their lively presenting skills on the Gem 106 breakfast show. They have been broadcasting together for over a decade since discovering their natural chemistry at a previous radio station. The duo proved a force to be reckoned with when they beat top names including Graham Norton and Chris Evans to win the coveted Music Radio Personality category at the 2014 Radio Academy Awards. Their success has put them firmly on the radio map and led to stand-in spots on BBC Radio 2.

Sam and Amy are huge foodie fans... Amy is a keen baker who finds whipping up cakes a therapeutic pastime and often posts recipes on her blog.

Sam, on the other hand, claims to be useless in the kitchen but cites this fisherman's pie recipe as his signature 'soul' dish, which he perfected during his bachelor years. Serves 4 (or probably just two massively manly fishermen).

Follow Sam and Amy on Twitter for recipes and foodie insights:
@amyvoce and @sampinkham.

## Ingredients

2 cod loins

2 salmon fillets

2 haddock fillets

A bag of the biggest (uncooked) prawns you can find!

6 large potatoes

4 eggs

2 beef tomatoes

Slab of mature cheddar cheese

Salt and pepper

Fresh asparagus and broccoli

**For the cheese sauce:**

75g butter

125g plain flour

470ml full fat milk

125g mature cheddar

Pinch of salt

2 twists of black pepper

## Method

First peel and chop your spuds and get them on the boil. Hard boil the eggs for around 9 minutes, then let them cool in a pan of cold water.

While the spuds are bubbling away cut the cod, salmon and haddock into manly-sized chunks then add it all, including the prawns, to an oven dish.

Next, make your cheese sauce. Start by melting the butter in a pan then add flour until it forms a smooth paste. Gradually stir in the milk until it becomes a smooth sauce then simmer for about a minute to reduce the milk. Add the cheese until it has completely melted, then add a manly amount of salt and pepper. BOOM! Manly and massively calorific cheese sauce!

Pour the sauce sparingly over the uncooked fish. Slice the eggs and beef tomatoes and layer them on top of the fish and sauce mix. Mash the potatoes with plenty of butter and spread the mash, about an inch thick, over the egg and tomato.

Grate a serious amount of mature cheddar cheese all over your pie and whack it in the oven at 190°c for 40 minutes.

Boil or steam your broccoli and asparagus so that they are ready for when the pie is done.

Serve your Massively Manly Fisherman's Pie with the asparagus, broccoli and at least one bottle of wine, then fall asleep in front of a log fire with a dog at your feet.

# *Quality* CLASSICS

A stones-throw apart, The Devonshire Arms at Beeley and
The Devonshire Arms at Pilsley have a unique identity and a different offering.

Devonshire Hotels & Restaurants is a collection of unique establishments in unspoiled locations across Derbyshire and Yorkshire, all part of the Duke of Devonshire's estate.

Alan Hill, from Chapel, has been chef patron at the Devonshire Arms in Beeley and its namesake in Pilsley for almost ten years. After previous experience at noted restaurants including the Michelin-starred Box Tree in Ilkley and Juniper in Manchester, the two Chatsworth estate restaurants provided him with a new challenge.

Both celebrate the abundance of quality produce Derbyshire offers and are among the few places where diners can enjoy eating meat reared on the estate. Many of the ingredients come directly from Chatsworth's Farm Shop, with other produce sourced within a 20 mile radius.

The Devonshire at Beeley is a picturesque country inn at the heart of village life. A hostelry has stood on the site since the 1600s when Beeley was on the main road north from London – first mention of the village was made in the Domesday Book of 1086.

Its historic charm merges seamlessly with the contemporary brasserie. The creative seasonal menu comprises classics such as fish & chips and steak au poivre, and more modern dishes including sticky pork belly with liquorice-infused carrots, and harissa spiced cod loin. Its Malt Vault area also offers a table for 12 diners to enjoy a private celebration.

An extensive wine list is available alongside a good selection of real ales from breweries including Peak Ales, just up the road.

This focus on quality local food and drink is also reflected at their sister pub. The Devonshire Arms at Pilsley has its own unique character and homely feel. The inn specialises in warm hospitality and a relaxed atmosphere – think pie and a pint by a roaring log fire.

The menu serves pub classics such as fish pie, corned beef hash and pan fried lambs liver; Sunday roasts and regular curry nights are also popular dining options.

With 14 chic, comfortable bedrooms at Beeley and 13 at Pilsley – all designed personally by the Duchess of Devonshire – there's even the chance to book in and make a night of it.

## From The FARMSHOP — PRICE

### PRODUCED ON THE CHATSWORTH ESTATE

- CURED BACON £13·95 PER KILO
- SAUSAGE £7·25 PER KILO
- LAMB CUTLETS £13·50 PER KILO
- MINUTE STEAK £10·95 PER KILO
- BLACK PUDDING £1·50 PER KILO

- ANDRÉ'S VINAIGRETTE £3·99 · 250g

- VINTAGE DARK ORANGE MARMALADE £2·99 · 340g

- LIME MARMALADE WITH PINEAPPLE £2·99 · 340g

ALL CAN BE PURCHASED
* FROM THE FARM SHOP *

# Devonshire Arms Beeley
## SLOW BRAISED STICKY PORK

With liquorice carrots, apple gnocchi and pak choi. Serves 6.

## Ingredients

**For the pork belly (day one)**

2kg belly pork, rind on

3 star anise

1 tbsp fennel seeds

1 tsp Sichuan pepper

5cm cinnamon stick

½ tsp dried chilli flakes

30 garlic cloves, chopped

50g sea salt

2 tbsp sesame or olive oil

**For the cooking liquor (day two)**

2 litres veal stock

350ml good quality soy sauce

1 tbsp redcurrant jelly

75ml balsamic vinegar

175ml dry sherry or sake

**For the glaze (day three)**

4 tbsp soft brown sugar

130ml water

1 tbsp dark soy sauce

1 tsp ground five spice

1 tsp pomegranate molasses

**For the gnocchi**

170g type 00 flour

1 whole egg

2 egg yolks

2 large russet potatoes

1 tsp fresh nutmeg

Pinch of salt

1 Bramley apple, diced and cooked

**For the carrot purée**

360g carrots

300ml chicken stock

20g caster sugar

½ liquorice stick

2 sprigs thyme

240g unsalted butter

Salt and pepper, to season

**For the liquorice carrots**

450g heritage carrots

1 tsp cumin seeds

1 tsp orange zest

1 liquorice stick

4 tbsp good quality olive oil

Pinch of sea salt

$^{1}/_{8}$ tsp sugar

250ml orange juice

Splash lemon juice

**To garnish**

Fried pak choi

Crackling

## Method

### For the pork belly

In a pestle and mortar grind up the fennel seeds, star anise, Sichuan pepper, cinnamon and chilli flakes. Add this to the salt and garlic, then mix together to make a rub.

Place the pork belly on a large tray, pour over a small amount of boiling water and set aside to cool – this will render the fat and allow the spices to penetrate the meat.

Add the rub mix and oil to the pork and massage it in to the meat. Leave to marinate in the fridge for 24 hours.

### For the cooking liquor

Heat the veal stock and soy sauce. Add the sherry and balasmic vinegar then simmer for 30 minutes. Stir in the redcurrant jelly until dissolved. Set aside.

To cook the pork belly, preheat the oven to 150°c. We use a sous-vide machine to cook the pork belly in our kitchen, but it can be done in the oven. Wash the pork belly with cold water to remove excess spice and salt and then dry it with a cloth.

Place the belly in a large tray and cover with cooking liquor, then wrap it in parchment paper and foil. Cook for 6 hours – when a thin skewer inserted into the meat offers no resistance, it is cooked. Remove from the oven and cool in the liquor.

Save some of the liquor, reduce by two thirds and put to one side.

Once cool remove the pork and place on a tray with a weighted tray on top to press the pork flat. Leave overnight to set.

### For the sticky glaze

Place sugar in a dry pan on a low heat until it becomes a light caramel. Add water to hot caramel (take care as it will boil vigorously) and simmer until all the sugar has dissolved and you're left with a syrup.

Add the rest of the ingredients and stir until the spices are dissolved. Chill until needed.

### For the gnocchi

Boil the potatoes whole for around 45 minutes until soft. Peel and pass through a vegetable mill while still warm, then through a drum sieve. Place the mashed potato on to a clean pasta board.

Make a well in the centre of the potatoes and sprinkle all the flour over. Place the eggs, apple, nutmeg and salt in the well and stir into the flour and potatoes using a fork.

Bring the dough together, kneading gently until a ball is formed. Knead for another 4 minutes until the ball is dry to touch.

Roll tennis ball-sized pieces of dough into 2cm diameter dowels and cut into 2cm long pieces. Drop the pieces into boiling water and cook for around 5 minutes until they float.

### For the carrot purée

Peel the carrots and place on a tray in a single layer. Add the chicken stock, sugar, thyme, liquorice, half of the butter, salt and pepper. Cover tightly with foil, bring to a boil then bake in oven at 180°c for 25 minutes or until soft and the liquid has evaporated. Liquidise until silky smooth before slowly adding the remaining butter. Correct the consistency by adding warm water. Season to taste and chill.

### For the liquorice carrots

Peel and trim carrots, then scoop then out with a Parissien cutter. Place in a stainless steel pan, large enough to fit them in a single layer. Add the cumin, orange zest, liquorice, oil, salt, sugar and orange juice. Bring to the boil, stirring well, then add the carrots. Cover and simmer gently until carrots are tender. Add lemon juice and chill.

### Assembly

Remove pork belly from the press, trim the edges and cut into two 10cm rectangles.

In a hot pan sear the pork belly, rind side down, until crispy.

Remove from the pan and place on a tray lined with greaseproof paper. Using a paint brush cover the pork with the glaze, cook in the oven at 180°c for 12 minutes, then rest for 2 minutes in a warm place.

In a hot pan shallow fry the gnocchi until golden and crispy.

Heat the carrots and carrot purée taking care not to over-reduce the purée.

Dress the plate with the pork in the centre on a swoosh of purée. Dot the carrots and gnocchi around, pour over the reduced liquor and garnish with fried pak choi and crackling.

# Devonshire Arms Pilsley
## BEEF COBBLER

With anchovy and caper butter. Serves 4.

## Ingredients

**For the casserole:**

1kg diced stewing beef

2 tbsp vegetable oil

200g carrots, diced

200g Spanish onions

1 stick celery, diced

200g swede, diced

1 sprig thyme, leaves only

2 pints beef stock

Tomato purée

Salt

Pepper

**For the herb scone:**

200g self-raising flour

40g unsalted butter

1 dessert spoon mixed herbs (chives, basil, tarragon and thyme)

Salt

Pepper

Milk to bind

**For the anchovy and caper butter:**

100g unsalted butter, softened

2 anchovy fillets, chopped

40g baby capers, rinsed and chopped

1 tsp parsley and chives, chopped

## Method

**For the casserole**

In a thick-bottomed saucepan heat the oil until hot. Add the beef and brown on all sides.

Add the carrots, onions, celery and swede and cook for five minutes then put in the thyme and a squeeze of tomato purée and stir.

Pour in the beef stock and slowly bring to the boil. Turn the heat down and allow the beef casserole to cook slowly for around 2 hours or until tender. Season with salt and pepper to taste.

**For the herb scone**

Preheat the oven to 180°c.

Put the flour and butter in a bowl and rub together with your fingertips until the mixture resembles breadcrumbs. Add the herbs, salt and pepper and mix evenly.

Bind the mixture by adding a little milk at a time until a pastry has formed. Wrap the scone mix in cling film and place in the fridge for 20 minutes.

Once rested, roll out to roughly 6mm thick. Cut into circles approximately 5cm in diameter. Place on a greased baking tray and bake for 15-20 minutes.

**For the anchovy and caper butter**

Place all ingredients in a bowl and mix with a wooden spoon.

**To serve**

When the casserole is cooked, place into a serving dish. Arrange the scones on top, with a generous amount of caper and anchovy butter on each. Place in the oven to melt the butter then serve.

# The best in
# LOCAL PRODUCE

Morley Hayes' prestigious Dovecote Restaurant has a host of regional accolades – as well as a picturesque rural setting.

Morley Hayes is a beautiful complex housing a hotel, restaurants, business and wedding facilities and a golf course – but it started life as a Derbyshire farm.

Brothers Andrew and Robert Allsop gradually developed the farm, converting outhouses and barns into appealing sociable spaces.

Roosters Bar & Restaurant provided the first food offering, specialising in home-cooked fare. It was followed by Dovecote Restaurant – a characterful converted barn with modern decor – for fine dining and occasions. At the same time, the surrounding farmland became an 18-hole championship length golf course.

Dovecote Restaurant, which opened in 1991, now boasts two AA Rosettes. It also won Restaurant of the Year at the Derbyshire Food & Drink Awards in 2012, and Best Out of Town Restaurant a year later at the Derby Food & Drink Awards, putting Morley Hayes firmly on the map as a destination venue.

Elements of the menus change fortnightly to reflect the seasons and use quality local produce. Dishes comprise of classics with a modern touch and occasional global inspiration; think pheasant with Jerusalem artichoke purée; Colton Bassett Stilton & pear tart tatin; soy-glazed fillet of mackerel with a macadamia nut crumb.

Dovecote Classics are popular features, offering diners traditional options at excellent value. Regular dishes include chicken liver parfait, fisherman's pie and lemon posset.

Meat comes from butchers Owen Taylor in Alfreton; with some beef from Dexter cattle on the Allsops' farm, as do their quails' eggs.

With milk and cream from the local Duffield Dairy, and vegetables from Zest Produce in Little Eaton, building relationships with trusted suppliers has been key at Morley Hayes since day one and many are named on the restaurant's menus.

Champagne breakfast, Sunday lunch and afternoon tea are popular options, complementing the set price lunch and full à la carte menus.

The new Hayloft room offers space for private dining with views over the golf course and is perfect for intimate dining, dinner parties, weddings and celebrations.

# Dovecote Restaurant
## SEA TROUT

With Melbourne asparagus, crushed Jersey Royals
and pink grapefruit butter sauce. Serves 4.

## Ingredients

4 x 170g sea trout fillets

600g Jersey Royal potatoes

50g butter

Punnet of pea shoots

70g samphire

2 bunches asparagus

4 radishes, sliced

Oil, for frying

Salt and pepper

**For the lemon crumb:**

30g butter

60g breadcrumbs

1 lemon, zested

**For the sauce:**

125ml white wine

40ml white wine vinegar

130g good quality cold butter, diced

15g shallots, diced

2 pink grapefruits, segmented

Dessert spoon parsley, finely chopped

## Method

### To make the lemon crumb

Lightly fry the breadcrumbs in the butter until golden brown, then add the lemon zest. Set aside.

Wash and boil the potatoes, leaving the skins on. Once cooked, peel and crush with 50g of butter and season with salt and pepper.

### For the sauce

Sweat off the shallots in a little butter. Add the white wine and vinegar and simmer until reduced by two thirds. Whisk in the butter one piece at a time. Put to one side at room temperature until required.

Season the sea trout fillets and heat the oil in a frying pan.

Lay the fillets presentation-side down in the pan and cook for 4-5 minutes or until golden brown.

Blanch the asparagus in a pan of boiling salted water for 2 minutes, adding the samphire for the last minute. Season with salt and pepper

To finish the sauce add half of the pink grapefruit – keeping the best segments for presentation – and the chopped parsley. Whisk them in over a low heat, otherwise the sauce will split.

### To serve

When the sea trout, potatoes, asparagus, sauce and samphire are all hot it's time to start plating; first place the sea trout on the plate followed by crushed potatoes, asparagus and sauce, then the samphire. Place two grapefruit segments on the fish. Garnish with radishes and pea shoots and serve.

# Dining with THE STARS

Attaining a Michelin star is a great achievement –
retaining your Michelin star for 21 years is simply amazing!

Fischer's restaurant at Baslow Hall reached an impressive milestone in 2015 when it retained Michelin Star status for the 21st consecutive year.

The first star was awarded under chef patron Max Fischer in 1994 thanks to foundations he built with wife and business partner Susan. The honour, along with three AA Rosettes, Good Food Guide listings and many more accolades, has been retained by current head chef Rupert Rowley who joined them 13 years ago.

Rupert and his team cook with the seasons. The majority of the produce they use is British and some is sourced nearby from suppliers including Brock & Morton rapeseed oil at Ashford-In-The-Water and the Sheffield Honey Company, which has installed bee hives on the Hall's grounds. Dishes are served on hand-thrown stoneware plates made in the village at Baslow Pottery.

The Fischer's kitchen garden is also a source of produce including a variety of fruits, vegetables and herbs, which are picked as required by the chefs.

For those wanting to dip their toe in the waters of Michelin starred dining, the Taste of Britain lunch menu is the perfect option. It features fresh, seasonal British ingredients used with Rupert's classical approach that also combines modern techniques and European influences. Yorkshire game and bread flavoured with local ales have been past features.

Diners can now experience this impressive cooking on a more intimate level with the introduction of an exclusive kitchen dining opportunity. Small groups can book in at limited times for a friendly, personal tour with Rupert and his team as they prepare and create a tasting menu in the heart of the newly renovated kitchen. A stroll round the kitchen gardens will also be available in warmer months.

Baslow Hall has been lovingly restored by Susan and Max since they fell in love with it back in 1988. As well as the restaurant, the hall boasts six guest bedrooms in the main building and five in the garden house, along with facilities for private dining, business meetings and intimate weddings.

# Fischer's
# HONEYCOMB PARFAIT

With strawberries, lemon verbena financier and milk. Serves 10.

## Ingredients

**For the honeycomb:**

325g sugar

50ml honey

125ml glucose

60ml water

15g bicarbonate of soda

**For the parfait:**

125ml milk

75g honeycomb

80ml egg yolk

200ml double cream

12.5g ice cream stabiliser

**For the financier:**

100g flour

100g caster sugar

100g ground almonds

150g icing sugar

250ml beurre noisette

240ml egg white

Dried or fresh lemon verbena

**For the milk honey tuile:**

200ml semi skimmed milk

2 tsp honey

Ultratex

**For the milk and honey ice cream:**

1750ml milk reduced to 1000ml

1 tin condensed milk

30ml honey

30g stabiliser

**For the lemon verbena gel:**

300ml water

150g sugar

20g dried lemon verbena

1 lemon, juiced

Ultratex

**To serve**

1 Punnet strawberries

Local honey

Minus 8 ice wine vinegar

Micro sorrel

## Method

**For the honeycomb**

Heat the ingredients in a large saucepan to a golden brown and then add the bicarbonate of soda. Whisk three times and carefully pour into a baking tray.

**For the parfait**

Warm the milk and add the honeycomb, then leave until it is fully dissolved.

Pour the milk over the egg yolks then return to the pan and cook until it thickens. Pour into a bowl and add the ice cream stabiliser with an electric hand mixer.

Lightly whip the cream and fold into the mix. Freeze immediately.

**For the financier**

Mix all of the dry ingredients and fold in the butter and egg whites when cooled. Fold in the lemon verbena and bake at 180°c.

**For the milk honey tuile**

Mix the milk and the honey together. Thicken with Ultratex until spreadable. Spread out on a mat and dehydrate until crisp.

**For the milk and honey ice cream**

Reduce the milk and mix all the other ingredients and churn in an ice cream machine until correct consistency.

**For the lemon verbena gel**

Bring all the ingredients to the boil and leave to infuse. Pass and thicken with Ultratex.

Serve with fresh strawberries macerated in honey, minus 8 ice wine vinegar and dots of vinegar thickened with Ultratex and micro sorrel.

# Made in Derbyshire
## BAKEWELL PUDDING

Derbyshire Record Office, based in Matlock, holds the historic archives that document 900 years of Derbyshire and Derby history. They include many household recipe books, or receipt books as they were known, dating back to the 17th Century. One example is the 1830s recipe book of Clara Palmer-Morewood of Alfreton Hall.

Recipe books of this time combine cookery recipes with medicinal and veterinary cures as well as beauty treatments. Clara's is a great example, with recipes for fashionable foreign dishes such as 'fromage fondue', 'petty shoes' (petit choux!) and 'Spanish fritters', but also 'a cure for dogs who are troubled with the snort', lip salve and a recipe to wash chintz amongst other delights.

Many of Clara's recipes have been contributed by friends and relations, whose names are given beside each recipe, so the book also gives an insight into Clara's social circle. You can see a full list of recipes and their contributors in the online catalogue at www.derbyshire.gov.uk/recordoffice

What really makes Clara's book a treasure, though, is that it has a recipe for Bakewell Pudding dated 1837. Bakewell Pudding is a famous local speciality that legend claims was invented by accident in the 1860s. Clara's book shows that this local legend can't be completely true... it is also a really delicious and easy recipe.

## Ingredients

**For the puff pastry:**

1 packet of ready-made puff pastry

**For the filling:**

2 tbsp raspberry/strawberry jam

1-2 tsp candied mixed peel (optional)

50g flaked almonds

4 egg yolks

1 egg white

100g butter, melted

100g sugar

## Method

Line an 18cm metal pie dish with puff pastry.

Spread the jam over the bottom and scatter over some candied orange peel, if you like it, and flaked almonds to taste.

As an alternative to jam you can use finely chopped dried cherries or raisins. Cherries are better as they are a bit more tart.

In a bowl put the egg yolks, egg white, cooled melted butter and sugar.

Beat for a couple of minutes with an electric whisk until fluffy, if you are whisking by hand it will take longer.

Pour into the pie dish and bake in the middle of the oven at 180˚c for 30-35 minutes.

# World CLASS

Iberico World Tapas offer globally-inspired food in a relaxed environment – perfect for the casual dinner, or indeed any special occasion.

Hot on the heels of its successful Nottingham sibling, Iberico World Tapas burst on to Derby's food scene determined to match it for quality, value and a coveted Michelin Bib Gourmand.

Owners Dan Lindsay and Jacque Ferreira – also the group's executive chef – achieved the award within a year of opening. The restaurant was also named Best Newcomer in the Derby Food & Drink Awards.

Iberico Derby is the only restaurant in Derbyshire to hold a Bib Gourmand, which has been a Michelin Guide certification since 1955 recognising 'exceptional good food at moderate prices' – something Iberico boasts by the plateful.

Housed in a light, airy Grade II listed former magistrates court, it incorporates laid back Spanish style and a buzzing atmosphere, which serve as a unique backdrop to Jacque's refined, quality cooking.

Here you can tuck in to perfectly executed tapas from around the world. There are hearty, traditional Spanish plates such

as rich lamb albondigas and plump chorizo cooked in Rioja, which deliver a punch to the tastebuds with big, robust flavours, full of depth.

These contrast beautifully with more delicate Asian influenced options, including spicy miso salmon and steamed edamame with Maldon sea salt, which give Jacque the perfect opportunity to showcase his background in Japanese cooking.

Charcuterie and cheeses are popular choices too – especially the restaurant's namesake, which comes from pigs fed on acorns and is considered the 'king of hams'.

The globally-inspired menu is complemented by a hand-picked wine list and comprehensive range of sherries. The latter might not seem the obvious accompaniment, but with characteristics from dry and nutty to sweet and syrupy, sherry can enhance a plethora of the seasonally led menu's dishes.

The relaxed, sociable sharing of food that has for so long been enjoyed on the Continent is finally here, and Iberico is the prime place to experience it.

Iberico World Tapas

# *Iberico's*
# LEMON AND GINGER CURED MACKEREL

With crushed edamame. Serves 2 as a sharing dish.

## Ingredients

1 mackerel fillet, de-boned with belly skin trimmed

250g table salt

300ml rice wine vinegar

150g sugar

2 tbsp coriander seeds, toasted

2 lemons, with zest cut into matchsticks

60g ginger, peeled and thinly sliced

30g edamame beans, steamed and podded

1 small red radish, thinly sliced

Olive oil

Salt, to season

Pea shoots to garnish

## Method

To make the cure, mix the rice wine, sugar and coriander seeds in a pan. Add the lemon zest and ginger.

Bring to the boil and simmer for a few minutes on a low heat.

Remove from the heat and cool completely, then put to one side. Reserve some of the lemon and ginger for garnish.

Cover the mackerel fillet in salt for 30 minutes to draw out some moisture, then rinse in cold water to remove the salt. Pat the fillet dry.

Next, add the fillet to the cure for 24-48 hours.

Once cured, the mackerel can be sliced thinly and arranged flat on a plate.

Season the edamame beans with olive oil and salt.

Arrange the edamame then place the lemon, ginger, thinly sliced radish and pea shoots on top then serve.

# Nothing to LOSE

Staying the night ... or staying for dinner?
Eitherway, you're in for a treat at Losehill House

Losehill House started life as a retreat for Edwardian ramblers and it could have ended up as a forgotten ruin if its potential had not been spotted...

The arts and crafts gem fell into dereliction after its business was hit by the foot-and-mouth outbreak of 2001. But it was later restored as a private hotel – and its future was finally secured when the current owners transformed it into a boutique spa hotel, seamlessly blending flourishes of contemporary chic with historical character.

Experienced hoteliers Paul and Kathryn Roden stumbled across the place in 2007 and immediately fell in love with it. Since then, they have incorporated a spa and the Orangery restaurant, which boasts beautiful countryside views on three sides.

Losehill House is the only four star spa hotel in the Peak District – and its award-winning restaurant holds two AA Rosettes and a Michelin Guide recommendation.

At the kitchen helm is passionate head chef Darren Goodwin, who "cooks the best the region has to offer in beautiful surroundings, no pretension."

His commitment to quality and provenance is unrivalled – the à la carte and tasting menus focus on flavour and technique and change daily, offering diners the opportunity to experience new dishes every visit.

Some produce is grown on site, including rhubarb, broad beans and herbs, while eggs, milk and honey are sourced in Derbyshire and the surrounding area. Meat comes from local butchers Price & Fretwell, from farms in the Chesterfield area.

Darren likes to provide new experiences and often includes goat dishes on his menus. "Young goat is relatively fat free, making it lean and healthy." he says. "It has a good strong flavour and is extremely popular with customers. It's definitely a conversation starter!"

The kitchen's loyal core team is also part of the restaurant's success; sous chef James Kohanzad and chefs de partie Alfie Olinski and Josh Hilton have been trained under Darren's watchful eye over the last few years.

Combine all of Losehill House's unique attributes and, whether you stay the night or visit for dinner, you're in for a treat.

Losehill House

# Losehill House

## OXTAIL SOUP

## Ingredients

**For the sofrito:**

25ml olive oil

1 onion

1 carrot

2 sticks celery

Thyme leaves

**For the oxtail terrine & consommé:**

2 oxtails (ask your butcher to cut them into manageable pieces)

1 onion

4 carrots

4 sticks celery

3 litres good, clear beef stock

1kg lean beef mince

**For the watercress caviar:**

250ml watercress juice

1.2g sodium alginate

250ml water

2.5g calcium chloride

Olive oil

**For the horseradish ice cream:**

180ml cream

90ml milk

2g salt

50g horseradish sauce

3 egg yolks

10g sugar

Watercress leaves

## Method

**For the Sofrito**

Wash, peel and finely dice the vegetables then cook slowly in the oil and thyme until they are slightly softened.

**For the oxtail terrine and consommé**

Brown the oxtail pieces in a frying pan, or over charcoal as we do.

In a pressure cooker sauté the vegetables until golden brown. Add the oxtail pieces and beef stock and break the beef mince into the stock.

Put the pressure cooker on a high heat until it comes up to the boil, seal with the lid and cook for 1½ hours.

Allow the pressure cooker to cool down and remove the lid. Now separate the oxtail meat from the mince, discard the mince and carefully strain the stock through a clean cloth and sieve. The stock should be completely clear and a rich brown colour.

Pick the oxtail meat, add the sofrito, season to taste and roll into a sausage between cling film. Chill in the fridge. Skim the fat off the stock.

**For the watercress caviar**

Using a hand blender mix the alginate into the watercress juice. Wash the blender thoroughly. Now blend the water and calcium together.

To finish the 'caviar' drop small amounts of the watercress into the calcium solution and leave for a few moments. Use a small sieve to lift out the pearls and rinse in a bowl of water. Then place the pearls in a bowl with a little olive oil.

**For the horseradish ice cream**

Heat the milk, cream and horseradish then whisk the eggs, sugar and salt. Gradually pour in the cream mix and whisk until everything is combined. Allow to cool and churn in an ice cream maker or over iced water. Place in freezer and whisk every 15 minutes until frozen.

To serve, slice the oxtail into 3cm slices and gently sauté on both sides to warm through.

Warm the consommé.

In a bowl place the diced root vegetables and the watercress caviar – try and keep it in the centre of the dish so you can hide it.

Place the oxtail on top, followed by a few watercress leaves and then a scoop of the ice cream. Present to the table and pour in the consommé. This should release all the caviar pearls into view.

**Tip: Sodium alginate and calcium chloride can be bought online**

# It's a
# FAMILY AFFAIR

Set in idyllic countryside, the Marsh Green Farm Shop & Café is a true showcase of great local produce, with even more to come.

Marsh Green Farm Shop & Café nestles amidst idyllic emerald fields on the edge of Ashover village.

Wendy and Ray Townsend took over in February 2015 – a huge change from the business they ran for over 20 years which specialised in the manufacture and wholesale of fishing tackle.

Joined by their daughter, Liz Brentnall, the challenge of something new appealed to this entrepreneurial family – and they have already stamped their mark on the farm shop, café and deli.

A new menu has been developed which includes a core range – such as homemade fishcakes and their popular Derbyshire Breakfast, featuring the eponymous oatcakes.

Their light bites list features sharing platters comprising of cheeses including Peakland White, made in Hartington, and continental meats from the shop's deli counter. Fresh baguettes, crackers, pickles and chutneys make the perfect accompaniments.

This is supplemented by a regularly changing specials board, which takes advantage of seasonal produce and other farm shop ingredients.

The family is also enhancing customer experience by building an on-site bakery, which they will run themselves following artisanal bakery training. A wide choice of quality baked goods will be available including breads and additional varieties of pies and pasties.

The farm shop is also home to long-standing Master Butcher Barry Anderssen. Barry, from South Africa, makes black pudding and biltong on the premises. His best-selling Boerewors – a popular South African sausage – are award-winners, as is his home-cured bacon, which attracts customers from miles around.

Additional meat is sourced locally and occasionally comes from English longhorn cattle grazing on the Marsh Green estate's 150 acres of grass parkland.

The shop's shelves also stock a comprehensive range of gluten free products, such as pasta, flour and biscuits.

Every effort is made to source from local independent producers in order to support other small businesses, affirming Marsh Green Farm Shop and Café's status as a true family affair.

Small Chocolate
lollies
£1.50

HALF BONE IN LAMB
SHOULDER

£8.50 Per kg

# Marsh Green's
# DERBYSHIRE BREAKFAST

Showcasing the best ingredients in the region – there's nothing finer than a cooked breakfast. Serves 1.

## Ingredients

225g fine oatmeal

225g whole wheat or plain flour

1 tsp salt

10g fresh yeast

845ml warm milk and water, half and half

1 tsp sugar

3 rashers of streaky bacon, smoked or unsmoked

1 egg

Pinch of black pepper

## Method

Combine the salt, flour and oatmeal.

Dissolve the yeast with a little warm liquid and add the sugar. Allow to become frothy.

Mix the dry ingredients with the yeast and the rest of warm liquid to make a batter.

Cover with clean cloth and leave in a warm place for 1 hour.

Bake on a well-greased griddle. Put enough batter onto the griddle to produce an oatcake to a diameter of your choice. Derbyshire Oatcakes are normally around six inches.

Turn oatcake after 2-3 minutes when the top appears dry and the underneath is golden brown. Cook for a further 2-3 minutes.

Pan fry your bacon in a little oil or grill if you prefer.

Fry the egg in a little oil, or serve poached or scrambled.

Arrange on a serving plate and sprinkle with a little cracked black pepper.

*Tip: We recommend coming in and letting us cook our Derbyshire Breakfast for you – that way you can try our butcher Barry's fantastic homemade black pudding with it too!*

# *Italian* INSPIRED

The finest ice cream from Derbyshire – inspired by family trips to Italy.

Masson Farm, in the historic spa town of Matlock, is run by Mick and Amanda Dakin with their children Jack and Josh – the third and fourth generations of the family to work there since 1930.

Mick was always keen to open their working dairy farm to the public to encourage greater understanding of how food gets from farm to fork – and their ice cream parlour and café have made that dream a reality.

Matlock Meadows ice cream was launched in 2011, inspired by gelato following a family trip to Italy. The family created its own version using high quality milk from their 90 Holstein Friesian cows.

Amanda makes the ice cream in small batches; flavours include red berry cheesecake and strawberry – created using local produce whenever possible – and 'Hokey Pokey' is rippled with Amanda's homemade cinder toffee. Both the chocolate and banoffee varieties have won awards from the National Ice Cream Alliance.

Many of the ice creams are gluten free and made to an Italian-style recipe, which gives a lower fat content and incorporates very little air for a dense, intensely flavoured dessert. The sweet treats can be enjoyed on site or taken home in a tub.

And visitors can indulge in more than just ice cream. The farm's coffee shop, open Friday to Sunday in the winter and daily except Mondays from March to October, serves a select menu: jacket potatoes, paninis, toasties and drinks are made using produce from the likes of E. W. Coates butchers in Darley Dale and Jacksons The Bakers in Clay Cross.

The farm also boasts an indoor viewing gallery in the milking parlour with disabled access, and rooms for parties, educational visits and meetings.

Visitors can meet a range of furry and feathered friends on the 200-acre farm, from calves in the hay barn to the Dakins' pet sheep, rabbits, chickens… and Pinky, the micro pig!

# Something for
# EVERYONE

Whether it's a chat over coffee, al fresco dining, or a more substantial Sunday 'arrosto' with family and friends – Nonna's has it all.

Nonna's exploded on to Chesterfield's food scene in 2009, giving the market town a stylish, versatile restaurant it had previously lacked.

The name was familiar to some locals thanks to its established sister site in Sheffield, but Chesterfield's own version is a refined individual. Located on the bustling Chatsworth Road, Nonna's is managed by Leonardo Prissi and Pasquale Palumbo, who have worked with founder Gian Bohan since the doors opened.

Nonna's floor-to-ceiling glass exterior sparkles enticingly to passers by – it's a shop window for the relaxed, stylish atmosphere to be found inside.

The urban-yet-polished interior is classy and warm; diners can delve into mouth-watering Italian classics, or more adventurous dishes on the seasonal à la carte menu, created by head chef Gavin Milligan. As much produce as possible is sourced from Derbyshire's rich larder, from milk to meat, herbs and beers.

Quality and value go hand-in-hand at Nonna's. Dine between 5pm and 7pm any day but Saturday and you can enjoy a bowl of handmade pasta and sauce for just £5.95.

Be it a relaxed brunch sipping mimosas, or a traditional-with-a-twist Sunday 'arrosto' with family and friends, there's a dish to tickle the tastebuds of every food lover. Food and drink can also be enjoyed al fresco in the warmer months on the outdoor terrace.

Upstairs, the bar's sumptuous interior provides the perfect backdrop for an evening of wine, craft beers and cocktails, offering plenty of opportunities to try something new. Classic Italian bitters and digestifs get star billing on the cocktail menu, brought bang up to date with a Nonna's twist – think Pasquale's grandmother's recipe for marinated cherries with a star anise and orange bitters flourish in lip smacking cocktail form.

And Nonna's is a popular daytime venue too. The coffee bar in the deli is a regular hubbub of chatter while friends share a drink and those on business conduct relaxed meetings over Italian coffee and biscotti.

Combine all this with live music, weekly themed food evenings, wedding hosting and outside catering – and it's clear that Nonna's offers something for everyone.

# Nonna's
# PAPPARDELLE DI ZUCCHINE CON CAPESANTE

Courgette pappardelle with seared scallops and crispy red mullet. Serves 4.

## Ingredients

2 large courgettes

12 scallops

2 fillets of mullet (½ fillet per person)

Lemon juice

Sea salt

Pepper

Extra virgin olive oil

½ clove garlic

3 handfuls of basil

100g Parmigiano Reggiano

110g pine nuts, lightly toasted

## Method

To make the pesto dressing place the garlic, basil, Parmigiano Reggiano, pine nuts and extra virgin olive oil in a food processor and whizz together to make a loose paste. Put to one side.

Cut the ends off the courgettes then peel into long strips – keep turning the vegetable so you get uniform strips.

Place the courgette pappardelle into a colander and dress with lemon juice, salt and a light dusting of pepper. Leave to drain for 8-10 minutes until softened.

In the meantime place a pan on medium high heat and add a tablespoon of oil to the pan. You want a really hot pan to achieve perfect searing.

Add your fillets of mullet skin side down and pan fry for 3 minutes, then remove and place on to a dish.

Lightly oil the pan again, return to a medium to high heat, then add scallops to the middle of the pan. Sear each side for 1½ minutes.

In a separate pan, warm your courgette through for around 2 minutes – no olive oil is required.

On a serving dish place your Pappardelle ribbons in clusters with three scallops spread around. Place a fillet of mullet on top of each cluster and finish the dish with the pesto dressing. Serve.

# Hands on HOSTS

Ali and husband Perry have the perfect blend of skills to ensure that Nourish at No.44 was a smash hit on the Derbyshire food scene.

When Ali Nadin's husband Perry moved to Belper from London after 15 years in some of the top restaurants and hotels, it didn't take him long to fall in love with his wife's native countryside.

The couple wanted to put down roots and continue their careers in hospitality; Ali's previous directorial role for a contract catering company and Perry's 30-year career as a classically trained chef meant a marriage of the perfect skills to run their own restaurant.

After a three-year search for the right place they stumbled upon the 16th century former Imperial Vaults pub in King Street. Extensive renovations transformed it into a bustling café by day and a shabby-chic candlelit bistro at night.

Nourish at No 44's floor-to-ceiling windows and al fresco tables in the 'secret garden' are a nod to café culture, enhanced by thoughtful wooden detail, exposed brickwork and clever mood lighting.

The couple are hands-on hosts: Ali leads the front-of-house team while Perry trains staff and leads the kitchen with a passion for local produce.

A mural behind the bar charts where ingredients are sourced: cakes from Emma's Cakes in Ripley, meat from the nearby Pig's Tale Farm Shop, fruit and veg from Belper's Fresh & Fruity. Coffee and tea are blended specially by Ardens in Chesterfield and strawberries, rhubarb and salad items often come from local allotments.

The Nadins' passion for produce is reflected in their menus. The à la carte features classical British dishes with a French or contemporary twist and a selection of world wines adds the perfect finishing touch.

Even the café menu shows attention to detail, with everything from a toasted croque madame and popular 'Hangover Benedict' to sandwiches, salads, biscuits and bread, all made on-site daily; dietary requirements can be catered for. This attention to detail has naturally brought acclaim with a Derbyshire Gold Taste Award.

Nourish also has ambitious plans for expansion upstairs with an additional 80 covers to meet demand and cookery school classes are also part of their bright future.

Nourish at No. 44

# Nourish at No. 44
# BEETROOT CURED SALMON

With goats' cheese truffles. Serves 4 as a starter course.

## Ingredients

**For the cured salmon:**

1 side of salmon, pin boned and trimmed

500g raw beetroot

6g fennel seeds

100g caster sugar

200g sea Salt

**For the goats' cheese truffles:**

100g goats' cheese

50g diced beetroot cured salmon

1 tsp grated fresh horseradish

**For the goats' cheese coatings:**

Finely chopped fresh chives

Dried fennel flower seeds

Dried ground liquorice root

## Method

Grate the beetroot and add the fennel seeds, caster sugar, and sea salt, then mix into a paste.

Cut the salmon in half and lay on a perforated tray with a solid base.

Evenly spread the paste over both halves of the salmon and sandwich together.

Cover with cling film and refrigerate for 10 hours.

Remove from the fridge, turn the salmon over, tip away any liquid and discard.

Cover with cling film again and leave in the refrigerator for another 20 hours.

Take out of the fridge, wash off any remaining paste, and pat dry.

Cling film and refrigerate until required. This can also be frozen in small batches to use in the future.

Combine the goats' cheese and diced cured salmon with the fresh horseradish and form into round balls.

Roll individual balls into any one of the three goats' cheese coatings.

Serve with a fresh herb salad.

# Roy McFarland's
## SEARED SEA BASS

With a bouillabaisse sauce, fennel dauphinoise and samphire. Serves 4.

Roy McFarland is one of the most respected figures in English football.
The former player and manager spent over 40 years in the game. He was described
by Brian Clough as 'a Rolls Royce of a defender', while former England manager
Kevin Keegan called him 'world class'.
Roy, or 'Super Mac' as he is known to fans, captained Derby County to win the Football League
Championship in 1972 and 1975, playing over 400 league games with them. He also led them
to the semi finals of the European Cup in 1973 under Brian Clough and Dave Mackay
and earned 28 caps for England.
Amongst others, Roy went on to manage Derby County from 1993-95, and fellow
Derbyshire team Chesterfield from 2003-2007.
Roy enjoys eating at Nourish at No. 44 and dines there regularly. The seared sea bass with
bouillabaisse sauce is one of his favourite dishes to eat from chef Perry Nadin's menu.

## Ingredients

170g-226g sea bass fillets

Samphire

**For the bouillabaisse sauce:**

40g butter

50ml olive oil

2 fennel bulbs

2 sticks of celery

1 white onion

1 carrot

2 red peppers

4 cloves garlic

2 litres of good fish stock

30g tomato paste

1 lemon zest

1kg plum tomatoes

50ml Pernod or Pastis

**For the fennel dauphinoise:**

1-2 fennel bulbs

400g waxy potatoes

220ml double cream

25g butter

100ml milk

2 sprigs thyme

1 tsp Dijon mustard

Seasoning

**For the rouille sauce:**

1 clove garlic

1 red pepper roasted and deseeded

1 tsp lemon juice

Salt and pepper

1 large egg yolk

200ml olive oil

## Method

### For the bouillabaisse sauce

Roughly chop the fennel, celery, onion, carrot and pepper.

Sweat the vegetables in the butter and oil.

Add all of the other ingredients and simmer for an hour and a half.

Pass through a fine sieve and season to taste.

### For the fennel dauphinoise

Using a mandolin thinly slice the fennel and potatoes.

Add the milk, cream, butter, thyme, mustard and seasoning in a pan and bring to the boil. Remove from the heat and set the liquid to one side.

In a square oven proof dish place a layer of potato, brush with a layer of the liquid and then layer the fennel on top. Again, brush with the liquid. Repeat these steps until all of the ingredients are used up.

Cover with parchment and then tightly wrap foil around the dish. Bake in the oven for an hour and a half at 150˚c.

### For the rouille sauce

Put the garlic, pepper, egg and lemon into a food processor and blend until smooth. Very slowly drizzle the oil whilst still processing on a very slow speed, until the mixture thickens.

Season to taste.

### To cook the sea bass and serve

Score the sea bass skin, season and fry in a hot pan for approximately 3-4 minutes, until the skin is crispy.

Serve the sea bass on the dauphinoise potatoes, pour over the bouillabaisse sauce and drizzle the rouille sauce onto the sea bass as a garnish.

Serve with the steamed samphire.

# Zena Hawley's
# RUSTIC DERBYSHIRE MUMCAKE

Zena Hawley is the Derby Telegraph's education correspondent. She lives in North Derbyshire and has been a journalist for 36 years.

Her family has a rich food heritage – Zena is the great great granddaughter of Joseph Wilson, who was responsible for selling the first famous Bakewell Puddings.

Culinary flair clearly runs in the family: Zena is at her happiest when spending time in the kitchen and regularly provides buffets for friends and family as well as for christenings and weddings.

"This dish is a recipe that has been passed down to me from my grandmother," she says. "It was jokingly referred to as 'mumcake' by her children, including my mum, and so the name has stuck with my two daughters as well."

The sweet recipe combines pastry, sponge, custard and fruit. When the custard sets, 'mumcake' can be eaten by hand as a slice of cake or as a dessert with cream, ice cream or more custard, either hot or cold.

Mumcake has a rustic look and originated in Derbyshire.

## Ingredients

**For the pastry:**

115g self-raising flour, sifted

55g butter, cut into pieces

2 tbsp water

**For the filling:**

450g cooking apples, peeled and sliced

2 egg yolks

60g caster sugar

25g plain white flour

1 vanilla pod

225ml milk

Pinch of salt

**For the sponge:**

115g caster sugar

115g butter

2 medium eggs

115g self-raising flour

Vanilla essence

Flaked almonds to decorate

## Method

Preheat the oven to 190°c.

Prepare the apples then place in a pan and cover with water. Heat them through on a moderate heat. Once softened set aside to cool.

Next, make the custard filling by beating together the egg yolks and sugar until thick and pale, then stir in the flour.

Slice open the vanilla pod and remove the small seeds. Place the milk in a heavy-bottomed saucepan together with the salt and vanilla seeds and bring to the boil. Remove from the heat. Whisk the milk into the egg mixture, then return it to the pan. Place over a low heat, whisking the contents constantly until the custard is thick and smooth. Set aside to cool.

Make the pastry by placing the flour and butter in a bowl. Rub it together with your fingertips until the mixture resembles fine breadcrumbs. Add sufficient water and work the mixture into a dough.

Flour a board and roll out a circle measuring about 20cm across. Place it in a pie or flan tin, ensuring it fits without stretching. Place a piece of greaseproof paper on the dough, add baking beans and bake blind in the oven for about 10 minutes. Remove and leave to cool.

Meanwhile prepare the sponge by beating the caster sugar and butter together in a bowl until well mixed. Add the two eggs, one at a time, and beat into the mixture ensuring plenty of air is mixed in. Fold in the flour and add two or three drops of vanilla essence.

To complete, remove the baking beans from the pastry and put the apple in, layering it neatly. Then spoon the custard mixture over the apples before finishing by adding the sponge mixture and smoothing it out to the edge of the pastry. Place the flaked almonds on top if desired.

Bake in the oven for about 35 minutes or until golden and firm to the touch. Remove and serve hot or cold with cream, custard or ice cream.

# The proof is in THE PUDDING

A fortunate accident gave birth to one of the most iconic puddings in the world – we're very thankful for that.

The Bakewell Pudding originated over 150 years ago, but few know that the famous dessert was created by accident. The Old Original Bakewell Pudding Shop sticks to the story that's has been passed down through the generations…

Annie Wilson lived with her husband Joseph, a candlestick maker, in the building that houses the current Pudding Shop.

Her friend Ann Greaves, the cook at the White Horse Inn (now the Rutland Arms), told how she once forgot to stir her egg mixture into the pastry and instead spread it on top of the jam in the pastry case. With nothing else to hand when some passing noblemen wanted a meal, she served it anyway – it went down a storm and the Bakewell Pudding was born.

Seeing its potential, Annie set up shop on the lower level of her house and went into business selling the dessert: a layer of sweet strawberry jam on a puff pastry base, topped with a mixture of eggs and almonds, which sets like a custard. But, showing entrepreneurial foresight, she kept one ingredient secret.

The secret is today protected by owner Jemma Beagrie, who started working in the shop over 16 years ago. She became manager in 2004, fell in love with new owner Nick Beagrie, and the couple now run a number of Derbyshire businesses together.

Recognising room for growth, the store was expanded to make space for a wide selection of local produce – from beers and cheeses, to jams, chutneys and artisan breads handmade at their Bakewell Bakery.

The upstairs restaurant and outdoor terrace serves traditional dishes, daily specials, afternoon tea and an extensive range of cakes.

A Bakewell Pudding Experience offers groups a chance to make their very own pudding, followed by either tea and coffee or a two course meal.

Puddings can be bought and posted anywhere in the world via the shop's website.

Warning: contents irresistible

# Old Bakewell Pudding Shop
## ORIGINAL BAKEWELL PUDDING

Serves 4-6 (6 small puddings or 2 large puddings)

## Ingredients

**For the puff pastry:**

225g plain flour

Pinch of salt

150ml cold water

180g butter

**For the pudding mix:**

4 tbsp seedless strawberry jam

250g unsalted butter

315g granulated sugar

3 medium eggs

15g ground almonds

Few drops of almond flavouring

Cream or custard to serve

## Method

Sieve together the flour and salt and rub in 30g of the butter. Gradually stir in the water until a soft dough forms. Wrap in cling film and chill in the fridge for 20 minutes.

Place the butter between two sheets of greaseproof paper and flatten out with a rolling pin to form a rectangle, roughly 10cm by 7.5cm.

Roll the dough out into another, larger rectangle, measuring 12.5cm by 25cm.

Take the butter out of the paper and place it on the dough. Fold the edges of the dough together to make an envelope and chill in the fridge for 10 minutes.

Roll the envelope out on a floured surface to make a rectangle three times longer than it is wide. Fold one third into the middle and then the other third on top. Seal the edges lightly with a rolling pin and turn the pastry 90 degrees.

Repeat the previous stage and place in the fridge to rest for 30 minutes.

Repeat the rolling and folding twice then put the dough in the fridge for another 30 minutes. Roll and fold two more times so the pastry will have been through the process six times altogether.

Now roll out and use as required.

For large puddings use Pyrex dishes about 5cm deep or big enough for a large dessert. For 4-6 smaller puddings use individual round tartlet dishes about 10cm by 2.5cm.

Line your dishes with a layer of your puff pastry.

Add a layer of strawberry jam to the pastry case.

Using hand beaters mix the butter on a medium speed until light and fluffy.

Fold the sugar, ground almonds and flavouring into the butter, then add the egg and beat for approximately 4 minutes on a slow speed.

Add the mixture on top of the jam in the pastry cases and bake at 200°c for 30 minutes or until golden.

Turn the oven off and leave the puddings to set with the oven door open for around 20 minutes before serving. Enjoy!

*Tips: To save time you could cheat and use frozen puff pastry.*

*Do not overfill your pastry case with pudding mixture as it is likely to boil out once it goes in the oven.*

# Not just run of THE MILL

With acclaim coming from all quarters, The Old Hall Inn & Paper Mill Inn have gone from strength-to-strength under the guidance of born-and-raised publican Dan Capper.

Dan Capper grew up living in the Old Hall at Whitehough, Chinley. The building – a 16th century coaching inn attached to Elizabethan Whitehough Hall – was bought by Dan's family in 1979.

They have twice leased the pub, but took back possession in 2007 when Dan decided to leave his job in London to return home and run operations. Dan has worked hard to restore the inn to the way he remembers it from childhood: as a thriving Derbyshire pub.

The Old Hall's popularity has grown so much that the Paper Mill Inn, just a short stroll across the road, was taken on in 2012 to run in tandem.

Both inns pride themselves on their constantly changing food and ale offering, which is epitomised in the popular steak and ale pudding. It's a simple but hearty dish made using top quality ingredients including fresh suet, local steak and beer from Bakewell's Thornbridge Brewery.

Food journalist Andrew Webb cited it in his Eat Britannia book as the best steak and ale pudding he had tried, and diners place orders for it when booking a table to avoid disappointment.

The focus on fresh, seasonal food continues throughout the menus. Beef bourguignon is served straight from the Old Hall's Aga, indulgent French Raclette can be enjoyed at a group banqueting table at Paper Mill Inn and lamb comes from the chef's farm in nearby King Sterndale.

The beer list encourages visitors to experience both pubs and their gardens, boasting brews from local producers as well as Belgian, German, Trappist and fruit beers and a huge range of English ciders. The Old Hall Inn has featured in the Good Beer Guide for many years, and has been shortlisted for 'Best Cask Pub in Britain' in the British Pub Awards numerous times.

The inns' beer and cider passion is further celebrated at their twice-annual beer and cider festivals, which are each attended by around 5,000 people.

Staying over is an option too, with eleven bedrooms between the two and a nearby self-catering cottage – the perfect place to relax after a Peak District walk with great food and drink in informal surroundings.

# Old Hall Inn's
# STEAK & ALE PUDDING

Serves 4.

## Ingredients

**For the filling:**

1 onion, diced

2 sprigs rosemary, chopped

Small handful thyme

600g chuck steak, diced

100g plain flour (50g to coat beef)

80g unsalted butter

2 pints real ale (we often use Thornbridge's Jaipur IPA)

500ml beef stock

**For the pastry:**

250g self-raising flour

125g beef suet

Pinch of salt

150ml water

## Method

Place the onion, rosemary and thyme into a deep pan and sweat off until the onion is translucent.

Coat the beef in flour and sear the meat until browned.

Place the meat into the pan with the onions and pour over your chosen ale and the beef stock. Bring to the boil and simmer for about 1½ hours. Keep checking to ensure there is always enough liquid in the pan.

Next, make a roux by melting equal amounts of butter and plain flour, stirring all the time. When meat is cooked, add the roux to the pan until the mixture thickens and put to one side.

Save some of the excess gravy for later to serve poured over the pudding or in a jug on the table.

To make the pastry, mix the flour, suet and salt in a deep bowl. Add the water and stir gently until combined – be careful not to over-mix as the suet will disappear into the pastry.

Roll out the pastry to just over ½cm thick.

Butter four 9cm pudding trays and line each with pastry, ensuring there are no tears or folds.

Fill each pudding tray to about three quarters full with mixture. Fold the pastry over, trimming any excess in the middle.

Wrap the puddings tightly in cling film, including their trays. Add them to the top layer of a steamer pan and bring to the boil.

Simmer for at least 40 minutes until ready to serve. We think they go perfectly with homemade chips, peas and a jug of the ale gravy.

Let's hope your guests have a heathy appetite!

# Poetry in MOTION

Rhyme nor reason would keep us away from the fantastic collection of ales on offer at The Old Poets' Corner.

A pub has existed on the site of the Old Poets' Corner since the 17th century. Originally a coaching inn, it burned down in the late 1890s and was rebuilt in its current mock-Tudor style.

Formerly known as The Red Lion, the pub became The Old Poets' Corner when owners Kim and Jackie Beresford took over in 2004.

Kim was born at Crich, trained as a chef, and became a beer aficionado while working at the Dead Poets Inn, Holbrook, so was keen to find a name that paid homage.

After digging through dusty records he stumbled across a picture of Leonard Wheatcroft, a 17th century poet and notorious womaniser, reading aloud to a crowd outside the pub. And so The Old Poets' Corner was born.

It has become a staple of village life, also drawing people from the surrounding areas thanks to its excellent reputation.

Drinkers can expect to find around 10 real ales on the bar, at least three from Ashover Brewery, Kim's other venture based in the old stables adjoining the pub. These are supplemented with guest beers, ciders, wines and spirits.

Hearty homemade fare has been a feature from day one – and there is not so much as a frozen chip in the kitchen. Food is locally sourced where possible and dishes are made from scratch, including locally-shot venison, meat and potato pies, stews and chillies.

The popular Derbyshire Breakfast uses hen, guinea fowl and duck eggs from poultry kept by Kim and Jackie. Sunday's curry night is another favourite and most weeks are a sell-out.

Guests can even stay overnight in one of the pub's five en-suite bedrooms.

Combined with a twice-annual beer festival, music and quiz evenings, and occasional themed food nights, it's easy to see why the Old Poets has become such a hit.

But just be wary if you venture into the basement – the room that still holds the old village mortuary slab has a reputation for ghostly goings-on…

# Old Poets' Corner
## BEER BATTERED HADDOCK

With homemade tartare sauce, chips and mushy peas. Serves 1.

## Ingredients

280g haddock fillet

Cooking oil, for deep frying

**For the beer batter:**

1 pint of light ale (we use our own Light Rale)

500g self-raising flour

Pinch of salt and pepper

**For the tartare sauce:**

200ml mayonnaise

3 tbsp capers, drained and chopped

3 tbsp gherkins, drained and chopped

1 small shallot, chopped

Squeeze of lemon juice

3 tbsp fresh parsley, chopped

Salt and freshly ground black pepper

## Method

To make the batter, place the self-raising flour into a large bowl and gradually whisk in the beer until thickened – it should resemble the consistency of double cream. Season with salt and pepper.

For the tartare sauce, mix all the ingredients together into a small bowl and serve straight away or store in the fridge until needed.

Preheat cooking oil to 180-190°c.

Flour both sides of the haddock fillet then dip in the batter mix until fully coated and carefully lower into the hot oil.

Deep fry in a pan for 8-10 minutes, or until golden brown and crisp. Remove from the pan and drain on kitchen paper.

Serve with chips, mushy peas and tartare sauce and garnish with a wedge of lemon.

# *Sheer* OPULENCE

Derby's first boutique hotel offers contemporary British cuisine
– Derby's best kept secret.

It is hard to believe that stylish Opulence is housed in what was formerly a plain constabulary and council building.

The site was bought by James Blick in 2007 and transformed with a £3million refurbishment to become Derby's first and foremost boutique hotel, incorporating Opulence Restaurant.

True to its name, Opulence's interior is impressive to behold. The grand sweeping staircase with original stained glass windows is a highlight, beautifully complemented by oak wall panelling, decorative ceilings and Italian glass chandeliers. An original mosaic floor and marble pillars complete the look.

While the style is contemporary British – reflected in Opulence's Michelin recommendation – the atmosphere is relaxed with a buzz of conversation.

The food is exciting, with a modern twist, beautifully presented with freshness and seasonality in mind. Locally sourced produce is a focus.

All dishes are cooked from scratch on site and presented by a front-of-house team delivering high standards of service. Menu highlights include raw and cooked asparagus and fried quails egg with Parmesan and truffle embellishments and a decadent chocolate and coconut pot.

Opulence also boasts the only chef's table in Derby – a unique area on the edge of the kitchen seating up to eight people. This enables diners to interact with the chefs while enjoying taster menus of six or eight courses.

There are two additional private dining rooms and Opulence prides itself on offering bespoke menus for every requirement.

A 150-bin wine list complements the menu, as well as beers and a cocktail bar.

Afternoon teas are a popular feature as are Champagne breakfasts, set lunches and early dining menus.

Opulence was among the final three contenders for the Derby Food and Drink Awards Restaurant of the Year in 2014 and also boasts the royal seal of approval: in 2010 the restaurant served lunch to the Queen.

# Opulence
## TASTE OF DERBYSHIRE PORK

With spring vegetables and apple. Serves 4.

## Ingredients

500g pork belly

1 pork fillet tender loin

1 George Stafford black pudding

2 large potatoes

1 packet baby vegetables

1 spring cabbage

1 Granny Smith apple

Pinch sugar

150ml pork stock

150ml apple juice

50ml double cream

150ml white wine

1 egg, beaten

100g butter

Small bunch of thyme

Salt and pepper

Micro herbs or soft herbs, for garnish

2 garlic cloves

Panko breadcrumbs

Plain flour

Vegetable oil, for deep frying

## Method

Season the pork belly with salt and pepper and place in a deep tray with 100ml of apple juice, pork stock, white wine, two garlic cloves and a sprig of thyme. Cover then braise at 150°c for 3 hours in the oven.

Cut the pork fillet into 1 inch medallions and set aside.

Break up the black pudding into a mixing bowl and combine with half of the beaten egg and season. Then roll into small balls and coat with flour, then egg and finish by rolling in breadcrumbs.

Cut the potatoes into four portions of your desired shape and cook in a mixture of 50ml white wine, 50g butter and a sprig of thyme. Cover with foil and cook at 160°c until just cooked – you should be able to easily slip a knife into the centre.

Blanch the baby vegetables in boiling water for 2 minutes, refresh in cold water then set aside.

Slice the cabbage finely and deep fry in vegetable oil for 20-30 seconds at 170°c and drain on kitchen roll, then set aside.

Cut the apple into small dice and cook in a pan with a little apple juice and a pinch of sugar until soft, then purée the mix in a blender.

When the belly pork is cooked, strain off the liquid into a pan and reduce by two thirds before adding the double cream, then reduce a little more to complete the sauce.

To finish the dish, lay out four plates of your choice, then sear the pork fillet and belly in the same pan and transfer to the oven at 180°c for 6 minutes.

Garnish with micro herbs.

Place the baby vegetables and potato fondant in a pan with a little butter and water and heat until piping hot. Glaze them sufficiently by coating them with the liquid inside the pan.

Deep fry the black pudding bon bons until golden brown.

Now gather all your components together on a tray and carefully arrange the ingredients on the plate in your own design. Start with the purée and the vegetables, then the potato and meat, finishing with the sauce and garnish.

# Down at the BUTCHERS

The way food gets from farm to fork is important to Owen Taylor's.

The striking blue facade of Owen Taylor's butchery on Leabrooks Main Road is not just a shop front. It's a window to the workings of a large-scale operation with a strong, trusted heritage.

The business was started by Owen Taylor in 1922 at Chestnut Farm in Somercotes. The family business supplied its own on-site abattoir, which in turn supplied its shops in nearby Leabrooks, Alfreton, Somercotes, Riddings and Ripley.

Owen Taylor's started to build its reputation for providing high quality, locally-sourced meats as well as homemade sausages, pies and cooked meats.

The business moved to its current site when it outgrew the family farm and Owen's youngest son, the late John Taylor, took over in 1977. He worked diligently to upgrade and expand the wholesale and contract catering elements and was succeeded by his son and current managing director Richard.

Richard was thrust into running the company after the sudden death of his father, but was well-equipped to take on the role after years of experience spent on the family farm and working in the butchery business from a young age.

Along with wife Jane, Richard has developed the company and expanded from a largely wholesale business to provide the retail and catering markets with high quality, locally sourced fresh meat and meat products. They supply a significant number of award-winning restaurants in Derbyshire and also have a strong public sector customer base.

The business now employs almost 140 staff from steak cutters to pie makers, maintenance specialists, drivers, sausage makers, bakers, office staff, butchers, packers, pickers and cleaners. They also have a fleet of 18 eye-catching refrigerated vans that are a familiar site all over the county.

The way food gets from farm to fork is important for Owen Taylor's. In days gone by, the Taylor's bred and fed their own stock. They have since moved on to source produce from high quality 'Farm Assured' suppliers throughout Derbyshire and the surrounding counties, some of whom they have worked with for over 60 years. All their beef is grass and grain fed and aged on the bone for 21-28 days, making sure the meat is tender and full of flavour.

As with the company's earlier days, they handpick the finest animals, which are slaughtered at local abattoirs to minimise stress and food miles. This gives Owen Taylor's full control of their products and their traceability from farm to plate.

The company's rigid ethical practice of sourcing meat from local, trusted farms, visited personally by Richard, has helped to build a foundation of trust among customers from the outset. Be it a restaurant chef or a family cooking at home, provenance as demonstrated through direct contact with farmers is a reassurance for all Owen Taylor's customers.

Quality meat doesn't get any better than this – a fact reflected in the business's accreditations. The factory is certified by the National Association of Catering Butchers, while meat carries the Red Tractor mark, the UK's largest food assurance scheme, the English Beef & Lamb Executive quality standard mark and the British Pork Executive standard. They are also a member of the Q Guild of Butchers, which represents the highest quality butchers and independent meat retailers in the UK, and denotes an exceptional level of service and quality.

And there's plenty of variety for customers. In addition to the British beef, game, veal, poultry, lamb, pork and free range eggs they stock continental deli meats and cheeses, and French specialities such as poussin and corn fed chicken.

Their meat also goes into their own award-winning creations, including sausages, burgers, pies and pasties, which are supplied to restaurants and the public alike.

The team can also source other specialist meats with just a day's notice. For those who can't travel to the Leabrooks shop, a private delivery service is available, making Owen Taylor's products extremely accessible.

Owen Taylor's efforts to source and supply quality produce certainly haven't gone unnoticed and they are the recipients of an ongoing, ever evolving string of awards for both their traditional and innovative products alike. They were crowned Supreme Champion when they won the best pie in the country award at the NEC in Birmingham for their Huntsman Pie by the National Food & Meat Traders Association and they also won Best Pork Product in the British Pork Executive's (BPEX) awards.

April 2015 saw Owen Taylor officially crowned the winner of England's Best Sirloin Steak at the EBLEX Quality Standard Mark Excellence Awards in London. Owen Taylor triumphed being the only company in the country to be finalist in all three categories of the competition. As well as winning the Overall Champion in the Best Sirloin Steak competition, at the same awards they also won the Best Added Value Steak category with the Denver Fire Steak and came in the top three finalists in the food service section with their 12 Inch Steak and Stilton Pie.

# Cooking the perfect
# OWEN TAYLOR STEAK

## Selecting your steak

Using a good quality product is vital. If you don't know of a good local butcher, look for the nearest with Q Guild accreditation. Q Guild represents the highest quality butchers in the UK; they are independently audited to ensure their business meets set standards of hygiene and quality.

Good beef should be a deep red colour and preferably with marbling – thin streaks of fat running through the meat. This melts when the steak is cooked making it flavoursome and succulent.

The age of the meat is also important; the hanging process develops the flavour and tenderises the meat. As a rule, 21 days as a minimum and 35 days as a maximum is a good range to go for.

Fillet Steak: the most lean and tender of all steaks, it cooks quickly and there is no waste. Fillet can be considered to have less flavour although it is one of the most expensive cuts.

Sirloin: great flavour but a little less tender than fillet. It is usually cut about a 2cm thick steak and has a layer of fat running along the top. Any marbling can make it tastier and more succulent.

Rump: a firmer texture than sirloin and often considered to have more flavour.

Rib Eye: a slightly rounded steak cut from the eye of the fore rib. They carry a little more fat than other steaks but have a wonderful flavour. A double rib eye on the bone is called côte de bœuf.

## Cooking your steak

Firstly, ensure your steak is at room temperature.

Immediately before cooking lightly oil your steak. Rapeseed or groundnut oils are best as they can withstand high temperatures without burning.

A good steak should only need a sprinkling of sea salt and black pepper. Don't season too early or it will draw the moisture out of the meat.

Pan frying is the best way to cook a steak. Always ensure the pan is red hot when you place your steaks in it. Don't put too many steaks in one pan as this will cause the temperature to drop and the steaks will stew in their own juices.

If your steak has a fat layer on the outside, place this side in the pan first and cook for 1 minute. This will render the fat, crisp it up and help flavour the meat. Next, place your steak flat in the pan and cook for about 2 minutes. Don't move the steak around as this can make the steak become charred on the outside. Turn over and repeat on the other side.

Remove the steak and leave it to rest on a warm plate for at least 5 minutes before serving – this allows the fibres of the meat to re-absorb the juices to optimise tenderness.

It is important to consider the size and weight of your steak when deciding on the cooking times. Your butcher should be able to help you with this for the steaks you have bought, but here are some guidelines:

## Cooking Times – times given for each side of the steak

| Steak | Thickness of steak | Blue | Rare | Medium Rare | Medium | Well Done |
|-------|------|------|------|-------------|--------|-----------|
| Fillet | 3cm | 1 ½ minutes | 2 ¼ minutes | 3 ¼ minutes | 4 minutes | 6 minutes |
| Sirloin | 2cm | 1 min | 1 ½ minutes | 2 minutes | 2 ¼ minutes | 5 minutes |
| Rump | 2cm | 1 min | 1 ½ minutes | 2 minutes | 2 ¼ minutes | 5 minutes |
| Rib Eye | 2cm | 1 min | 1 ½ minutes | 2 minutes | 2 ¼ minutes | 5 minutes |

# The perfect English
# COUNTRY PUB

Full of character, The Packhorse Inn is one of those great traditional pubs that just oozes history and comfort.

The Packhorse Inn has served as a watering hole for locals and travellers alike since 1787. Formerly two miners' cottages, it lies on an old packhorse route running from Chesterfield through Baslow to Little Longstone, before climbing up towards Peak District beauty spot Monsal Head.

The Inn is perfectly situated for those enjoying a day out rambling in the nearby countryside, cycling the Monsal Trail, or visiting a range of nearby attractions including Chatsworth House and Haddon Hall. It's a cosy retreat in the winter too thanks to comfortable furnishings and a roaring log fire.

Boasting an acknowledgement in the 2015 Good Beer Guide, The Packhorse is a haven for beer lovers. The bar features a varied selection including award-winning brews from Thornbridge Brewery, as well as the usual selection of wines and spirits.

Visitors can also settle in a snug corner and tuck into fresh, local food. The daily changing blackboard menu often features wild boar from nearby woodland and venison from Round Green Farm. Beef is reared two fields away and sourced from Critchlows Farm Shop in nearby Bakewell. There's even a quirky tapas menu featuring beef dripping and pork pie.

Sticking with a theme, cheeses come from the Hartington Cheese Shop, while bread and Bakewell Pudding is lovingly baked at the Original Bakewell Pudding Shop.

Food is served every day, beer flows plentifully and there's even a weekly quiz night to raise money for charity. The perfect English country pub.

# The Packhorse Inn
# SLOW COOKED WILD BOAR BELLY

With potato rosti, curly kale, pickled wild mushrooms and port reduction.
Serves 4.

## Ingredients

**For the boar belly:**

1.5kg wild boar belly

2 tsp sea salt

50ml Brock & Morten rapeseed oil

2 carrots

2 celery sticks

2 onions

6 garlic cloves

4 rosemary sprigs

6 peppercorns

2 bay leaves

**For the pickled wild mushrooms:**

200ml white wine vinegar

100ml water

1 tsp salt

1 tsp sugar

5 black peppercorns

1 bay leaf

2 garlic cloves, sliced

150ml rapeseed oil

4 sprigs tarragon

250g wild mushrooms

**For the potato rosti:**

2 large Maris Piper potatoes

Rapeseed oil

Butter

Ground black pepper, to season

Sea salt to season

**For the port reduction:**

Reserved boar stock

500ml port

4 sprigs thyme

Butter

**For the root veg crisps and kale:**

1 parsnip

1 sweet potato

Kale

Rapeseed oil, for deep frying

## Method

**For the boar belly**

Preheat the oven to 220°c.

Score the skin of the belly, making cuts 1cm apart, then rub in the oil and sea salt.

Roughly chop all the vegetables and spread in a roasting tray with the garlic, rosemary, peppercorns and bay leaves. Place the meat on top and roast for 30 minutes.

Remove the tray and fill with cold water half way up the meat. Cover with foil and return to the oven at 170°c for a further 3 hours, or until tender.

Drain off the stock and set aside. Using a flat tray and a couple of cans as a weight, press the belly and allow to cool.

Once cooled, trim the edges and cut into four squares. Return to the oven 15 minutes before serving.

**For the pickled wild mushrooms**

Place vinegar, water, salt, peppercorns, sugar, bay leaf and garlic in a pan and bring to the boil. Add mushrooms and cook through for around 10 minutes.

Remove the mushrooms with a slotted spoon. Place on a tea towel and leave to dry.

Add the mushrooms to a sterilised glass jar with chopped tarragon then cover with rapeseed oil. Cover tightly with lid.

**For the potato rosti**

Peel and parboil the potatoes until just softened. Allow to cool a little, grate coarsely then season.

Heat a glug of oil and a good knob of butter in a frying pan on a medium heat. Place a large metal ring in the pan and half fill with potato, pressing in with the back of a spoon.

Remove the ring, brown the rosti on both sides and transfer to a baking tray. Repeat for up to four rostis then roast for around 10 minutes.

**For the port reduction**

Drain off the fat from the boar stock, add the port and thyme and reduce until thickened and syrupy. To finish whisk in a knob of butter.

**For the root veg crisps and kale**

Peel the parsnip and potato, discard the peelings, then continue to peel down as far as possible.

Deep fry the peelings in rapeseed oil until almost cooked (they will continue to cook a little when removed). Drain on kitchen roll and lightly season.

Strip the leaves from the kale stalks and blanch for 2 minutes in salted water.

# The Plough SHARE

With two talented chefs at the helm, The Plough Inn was always going to be 'a must' on the Derbyshire culinary map.

The Plough Inn is a listed 16th century pub near Brackenfield on the edge of the Peak District National Park. A former farmhouse, it is run by business partners Anthony Spencer and Laura Kay.

Anthony, from Ashbourne, comes from a family of professional bakers who branched out and bought nearby Callow Hall, turning it into a restaurant and country house hotel.

Anthony caught the hospitality bug and went on to gain a catering qualification before giving in to wanderlust and working abroad in a busy kitchen in Zurich, Switzerland.

Via a catering company in Belgium, and the Lygon Arms at Broadway in the Cotswolds, he returned home to work in the family business – and met Laura when she became sous chef at Callow Hall in 2010.

The duo set their sights on running their own business and took over the Plough Inn in April 2012. Laura, from Mansfield, was previously a pastry chef at Michelin-starred Fischer's in Baslow and focuses on the pub's baked goods, desserts and celebration cakes.

She created the featured gooey chocolate pudding, which is served at the Plough with liquorice ice cream – unsurprisingly a best-seller.

Anthony takes care of the savoury courses, which take the form of pub fare with a more extensive modern British offering during the evening.

Traditional pies, fish and chips and burgers form the heart of the menu while roasted stuffed quail and belly pork sit alongside a variety of fish including sea bass, wild halibut, plaice, cod and home-smoked salmon.

Sunday roasts feature pork loins and whole sirloins, butchered in-house. Meat comes from Owen Taylor's butchers and Mansfield farmer David Boot. Wild garlic and nettles are foraged in season and some of the pub's vegetables are even grown on Laura's father's allotment.

A weekday lunch menu and specials board also run alongside the à la carte menu at this unmissable destination pub.

# The Plough Inn
# HOT GOOEY CHOCOLATE PUDDING

Makes 7 small or one large pudding.

## Ingredients

**For the pudding:**

125g plain flour

Pinch of salt

120g caster sugar

3 tsp baking powder

4 tbsp cocoa powder

250ml milk

85g unsalted butter, melted

2 eggs, beaten

1 tsp vanilla essence

**For the topping:**

185g soft brown sugar

2 tbsp cocoa powder

250ml boiling water

## Method

To make the pudding, sift together the flour, salt, sugar, baking powder and cocoa.

Add the milk, butter, eggs and vanilla then mix with hand beaters until combined. Divide equally between seven 200ml pudding moulds.

For the topping, combine the brown sugar and cocoa together in a bowl and sprinkle it over each of the puddings.

Pour the boiling water carefully and equally over the puddings and bake for 20-25 minutes at 180°c (175°c in a fan oven).

Serve straight from the oven with ice cream – we recommend liquorice flavour – or fresh cream.

*Tip: The puddings can be reheated in the microwave for one minute if you don't want to use them all at once.*

# Modern CLASSICS

Menu inspiration comes from the rolling pastures of Derbyshire; with local meat and produce readily available on the menu.

The Pointing Dog & Duck nestles on the riverside in the historic market town of Bakewell.

The bar and restaurant, created in a restored marble works, oozes character with its ancient beams, rustic timber-clad walls and atmospheric industrial lighting.

It also enjoys one of the best views in the town thanks to its premier location on the leafy banks of the river Wye, which offers a relaxing backdrop for diners and drinkers.

The Pointing Dog & Duck's menus take inspiration from the surrounding land and the finest ingredients.

Traditional dishes such as fish and chips and best British rib eye steak are complemented by global flavours including a Middle Eastern grill platter, sea bass fillet puttanesca and Malaysian chicken satay with peanut sauce.

A selection of gourmet pizzas are also available featuring inspired flavour combinations such as prosciutto and goat's cheese, Moroccan spiced lamb meatballs and Calabrese sausage and japaleño pepper.

Desserts are a decadent affair: Baked Alaska, sticky toffee pudding and a changing tart of the day are among crowd pleasers for diners with a sweet tooth.

Sunday roasts are a popular choice for visitors, offering two and three-course options for a set price. Roast sirloin of beef and shoulder of lamb, both from Derbyshire, and pork tomahawk are served with seasonal vegetables, Yorkshire puddings, duck fat roasties and rich red wine gravy.

A comprehensive drinks list is available to wash it all down – including cocktails, local ales and great wines by the bottle and glass.

There is also a Pointing Dog Wine Club for both enthusiasts and those interested in learning a little more about wine.

A sunny terrace for al fresco dining and blazing log burner in colder months makes the Pointing Dog & Duck an enjoyable drinking and dining experience all year round.

With sister sites in Cheadle Hulme and the popular Ecclesall Road, Sheffield – it's a good excuse to have a drive out this summer.

Pointing Dog & Duck

# Pointing Dog & Duck
## BAKED ALASKA

Serves 4.

## Ingredients

*Strawberry jam*

*Vanilla ice cream*

*Icing sugar, for dusting*

*Fresh mint sprig*

**For the cookie crumbs:**

*150g butter*

*150g caster sugar*

*180g plain flour*

*1g vanilla bean paste*

*7g cocoa powder*

**For the Italian meringue:**

*325g caster sugar*

*85ml cold water*

*200g egg whites*

*75g caster sugar*

## Method

To make the cookie crumbs, melt the butter and add in the caster sugar. Blend the sifted flour, vanilla bean paste and cocoa then mix all of the ingredients together. Spread thinly and evenly on a baking tray and bake at 180°c for 10-12 minutes. Once cooled, crush to a fine crumble by hand.

For the Italian meringue place the 325g of caster sugar into a thick-bottomed saucepan with the water and heat slowly.

Beat the egg whites and remainder of the sugar with an electric whisk until thick and fluffy.

When the sugar and water on the stove reaches 115°c, slowly pour it in to the meringue mix while continuing to stir.

Once all the ingredients are combined, continue to whisk until the mix is stiff and light. It will take around 10 minutes to reach the perfect consistency.

Next assemble your Baked Alaska. Fill a piping bag with your homemade meringue mixture and carefully cut the point to create an 8mm opening.

Pipe one circle of meringue onto the centre of a plate (approximately 75mm in diameter). Half fill the circle with cookie crumbs.

Layer a generous spoonful of strawberry jam on top of the cookie crumbs then place two large scoops of your favourite vanilla ice cream on top of the jam.

Using the piping bag in one continuous movement, pipe in an upward spiral around the ice cream, making sure you completely cover it.

Blow torch the meringue to create a crisp exterior.

To serve, place a sprig of fresh mint in to the top of the Baked Alaska and lightly dust the plate with icing sugar.

***Tip: A blow-torch and a piping bag are useful when creating this recipe.***

# Forever in SEASON

An emphasis on seasonal quality ingredients, with both classcial and innovative dishes, it's small wonder that Rowley's is a jewel in the heart of Derbyshire.

Rowley's at Baslow has developed a solid reputation amongst discerning diners for superb cooking and classy presentation.

Those in the know are aware it's the more relaxed, rustic sibling of Michelin-starred Fischer's at Baslow Hall. The pub, formerly the Prince of Wales, was taken over by the Hall's proprietors, Max and Susan Fischer, with business partner and executive head chef Rupert Rowley in 2006.

Rowley's has an idyllic setting on the edge of the famous Chatsworth Estate and has been transformed into a stylish bar and restaurant. Contemporary decor and comfortable furnishings have ensured it has become a well-loved destination for diners in Baslow and a favourite place for a spontaneous lunch for visitors to the Peak District.

With such reputable names at the helm it's no wonder Rowley's has become known for well executed, simple dishes that feature fresh, locally sourced ingredients. The partners have worked closely with head chef Jason Kendra to develop menus combining classics – such as terrines, risottos and slow-cooked dishes – with more innovative creations that all have a strong focus on quality.

A variety of special menus are also on offer, including a pie and pint supper and a quintessentially British afternoon tea.

Served Tuesday to Saturday, the elegant afternoon tea menu features handmade sandwiches, scones, cakes, desserts and speciality teas. It can be enjoyed in the airy terrace dining room or out on the terrace itself on a fine day – perfect for special occasions or an afternoon with friends.

Max himself can sporadically be found moonlighting at Rowley's, providing inspiration to the kitchen team. His passion for gardening and seasonal produce have been integral to the development of the restaurant's identity – qualities that have been recognised with recent accolades including being named Local Food Hero in the Derbyshire Food & Drink Awards and an honorary doctorate from Sheffield Hallam University.

# Rowley's LEMON TART

Serves 8-10.

## Ingredients

**For the sweet pastry**

500g flour

150g caster sugar

3 egg yolks

2 eggs

200g butter

**For the lemon tart mix**

8 lemons, juiced and zested

10 eggs

250g butter

500g caster sugar

## Method

**For the sweet pastry**

Rub the butter, sugar and flour until well mixed.

Whisk the eggs and two yolks together and add to the mix until a smooth dough is formed.

Place in the fridge for 1 hour to rest and firm up.

Butter a flan ring.

Roll out the pastry and place in the tart case, then line with cling film and fill with baking beans.

Bake at 180°c until the pastry is cooked. Remove the cling film and beans.

Take one egg yolk and brush it all around the inside of the pastry. Put back in the oven for 2 minutes until the egg is cooked – this will give you a protective layer to stop the pastry case leaking.

**For the lemon tart mix**

Mix the eggs, lemon and sugar together.

Melt the butter and add to the other mix.

Using a hand blender, emulsify the mix. Make sure it is warm; if it starts to cool it will split.

If it feels cold to the touch give it 20 seconds in the microwave to warm it up.

Preheat the oven to 100°c. Put the tart case in the oven and then, using a jug, fill it with the mix. Bake for 30-40 minutes. When there is no wobble to the tart it is cooked.

Remove from the oven and leave to cool.

# Quick like THE FOX

Go and seek out this unexpected jewel – you'll be glad you did.

The Samuel Fox's history is deeply rooted in the working village of Bradwell. It was once an evening boozer – one of four in the locale – but the modern day inn has blossomed into a destination restaurant with bedrooms under the watchful eye of chef patron James Duckett.

Surprisingly, all of the village's pubs are still open, which is something James attributes to each one's ability to diversify. With two AA Rosettes, Michelin and Good Food Guide recommendations, four en-suite boutique bedrooms and an excellent location, it's not hard to see The Samuel Fox's appeal.

Since James took over in late 2012 they've gained acclaim winning 'Best Newcomer' in the Derbyshire Food and Drink Awards and becoming one of only a few holders of a Taste Derbyshire Gold Award.

James has taken inspiration from the building and its surroundings when considering the direction in which to take his food. He has arrived at refined pub dining – dishes are beautifully executed with punchy, robust flavours, but the atmosphere is relaxed. This is a reflection of James's own tastes, drawing on his global cooking experiences in France, Holland, Spain and Australia.

Provenance is a top priority for James. He is a self-confessed 'fair weather forager' and seeks out nettles, elderflowers and wild garlic from nearby lanes for use in his creations. He also takes advice from neighbour Simon Bartholomew – owner of local business The Herb Table – who has an expert eye for what can be foraged from Derbyshire's abundant pantry.

Other local produce includes cheeses from Hartington and Buxton, and meat from Owen Taylor's butchers.

The restaurant menu changes every week and a £5-£10-£5 early bird offer runs Wednesday to Saturday featuring starters, mains and desserts. There is also a seven-course tasting menu, with matching wines, enabling diners to experience the tastes and flavours of The Samuel Fox in one sitting.

The team is tight-knit, with most members having been there since James took over. Front-of-house staff come from the village and surrounding areas and sous chef, Warren Donahue, followed James from Devon after undertaking previous work experience with him.

Go and seek out this unexpected jewel – you'll be glad you did.

# The Samuel Fox
# BRAISED BEEF CHEEKS IN RED WINE

With ox-tongue croquettes, violet potatoes and roasted root vegetables in pancetta parcels, Serves 4.

## Ingredients

4 beef cheeks

100g sliced pancetta

3-4 slices of cooked ox tongue, cut 25mm thick

1 medium onion

2 sticks celery

2 large carrots

1 large leek

4 violet or black potatoes

1 large Maris Piper potato

1 head garlic

Small bunch of thyme

1 bay leaf

500ml red wine (Renishaw Hall is perfect for this dish)

100ml port

2 litres beef stock

50ml dripping

100g breadcrumbs

2 eggs

Butter, milk and cream (small amounts)

Plain flour

Salt and ground black pepper

## Method

Trim excess fat, skin and sinew from beef cheeks – your butcher can do this for you.

Wash and peel root vegetables. Remove four outer layers of the leek, keeping them intact. Soak in cold water for an hour then rinse and drain.

Cut carrots and celery into batons 10cm long and ½cm thick. Chop onions and put to one side with remaining leek and trimmings from carrots and celery.

Pour a little dripping into a large heavy pan. Heat, then add beef cheeks and brown on both sides until dark caramel in colour. Remove and place in a large casserole dish.

Add chopped onions to the pan with leek heart, garlic and root vegetable trimmings (keeping half the carrot for the purée); fry until brown. Sieve to discard dripping, return vegetables to pan, pour in wine and port and boil to reduce by half. Add to casserole with stock, bay leaf and thyme. Cover and cook at 150°c for around 4 hours until the beef is tender.

During this time bake the Maris Piper potato for around 90 minutes until soft; set aside to cool.

Leave beef cheeks to cool then remove from sauce and place on a tray. Pass sauce through a sieve to strain off vegetables and herbs, then replace on stove and reduce until thick and shiny, skimming off any impurities. Replace beef cheeks in sauce.

Using a small pastry cutter, cut eight discs from the ox tongue and set aside. Finely chop remaining tongue for the croquettes.

Bring violet potatoes to the boil in a pan of salted water and cook until tender. Drain and remove skin while still hot – you may need rubber gloves! Add boiling salted water to another deep pan and keep on the boil. Pour a bowl of water and ice cubes (ready to cool vegetables and stop the cooking process). Blanch the outer layers of leek in boiling water for 30 seconds then plunge into iced water. Repeat with celery and carrot batons, blanching for two minutes. When cold remove all vegetables from iced water and place on a cloth.

To prepare vegetable parcels, trim one of the leek layers to form a 4cm x 12cm rectangle. Place two pieces of celery and carrot on leek in a neat bundle and roll up tightly, then roll inside a strip of pancetta, tucking in the ends. Repeat to make four vegetable parcels.

Mash baked Maris Piper potato with a little butter, salt, pepper, thyme and chopped tongue. Roll into sausage shapes and cut into four cylinders 5cm long. In a bowl whisk two eggs and a drop of milk. Place flour in another bowl with a few pinches of salt and in a third bowl add breadcrumbs. Using a fork, roll the potato in flour, then egg wash and finally breadcrumbs. Place the croquettes on a tray.

Fry the carrot trimmings gently in a knob of butter and a pinch of salt until golden and soft; cover with milk and a touch of cream and reduce until thick. Blend until shiny and smooth then place purée in a small pan.

To compile the dish, heat beef cheeks in the sauce and add tongue discs. Fry vegetable parcels and croquettes in a little dripping until golden, then place on a baking tray with the violet potatoes. Place tray in oven at 180°c for 5 minutes.

Spread a spoonful of carrot purée over one half of a plate. Place beef cheek on the other half then position a vegetable parcel at the bottom and a croquette at the top of plate. Break up violet potatoes into rough pieces, season, then place roughly on top of the carrot purée. Add a couple of tongue discs to each plate then cover beef cheek in some of the sauce.

If you wish, add a garnish of baby carrots and sprinkle a herb crust by blitzing stale bread with parsley leaves. Enjoy with a glass of red wine!

*Tips: Violet potatoes are flavoursome and add visual impact, but a firm waxy potato such as a Charlotte will do. We cook our own ox tongue with root vegetables, garlic and thyme, but pre-prepared ox tongue from your butcher is fine as a whole tongue would be surplus to requirements!*

# The traditional SCOTSMAN

The Scotsman's Pack has offered a hearty welcome to travellers from North of the border, and elsewhere, since the 18th century.

Taking on The Scotsman's Pack at Hathersage fulfilled Nick Beagrie's ambition to become his own boss.

With a background in running pubs and clubs around Sheffield, Nick had the opportunity to purchase the pub's lease in 2002 and jumped at the chance to invest in a piece of history.

The pub stands on one of the old track roads that led to Sheffield before the 18th century. It served as a regular watering hole for 'packmen' along the route, who visited every farm and village in the area to offer goods and deliver news. Packmen from Scotland were known to have sold tweeds there to local farmers.

Nick has worked hard to restore the pub, including the renovation of its five en-suite guest bedrooms, which are popular with walkers. He and wife Jemma constantly strive to improve and update the pub's offering alongside their other businesses including The Old Bakewell Pudding Shop and the newly-acquired Eyre Arms at Calver.

The pub's menu has featured freshly cooked traditional fare ever since Nick took over. Executive chef Greg Goodison maintains the standard, combining a passion for quality fresh food with a wealth of experience.

An award-winning steak pie and lamb shank shepherd's pie are favourites with diners – both use premium meat from local suppliers.

Tempting cakes and desserts come from the Bakewell Bakery, which the Beagries also run, and there is always a selection of six cask ales on the bar, plus a range of wines available by the bottle or glass.

The pub submerges itself in village life – it gets involved in the annual carnival gala and is a popular refreshment spot for Hathersage's running club, while many of its staff live in the village. It even claims to house the chair of Little John, a legendary fellow outlaw of Robin Hood.

Fuse all this with log fires and typical English pub decor, and it's easy to see why The Scotsman's Pack is as popular now as it was with the old packmen.

# The Scotsman's Pack

## STEAK PIE

Serves 6.

## Ingredients

### For the pie mix:

900g stewing steak from your local butcher, cut into cubes

Plain flour, seasoned with salt for dusting

2 white onions, sliced

1 tbsp fresh thyme, chopped

Salt and freshly ground black pepper

1 pint hot beef stock

10ml Henderson's Relish

1 tsp English mustard

½ pint of local ale

5ml sunflower oil

### For the shortcrust pastry:

225g plain flour

100g unsalted butter

Pinch of salt

2-3 tbsp cold water

1 tsp wholegrain mustard

1 egg, beaten (for brushing)

## Method

### For the pastry:

Sieve the flour into large bowl. Chop the butter into cubes and rub together with the flour using your fingertips until the mixture resembles breadcrumbs.

Add the salt, water and mustard to make firm dough. Wrap the dough in cling film and chill in the fridge while preparing the pie filling.

### For the filling:

Dust the steak with the seasoned flour.

Heat the oil in a large pan and fry the meat until browned on all sides.

Add the onions, salt, pepper, mustard, thyme, ale and Henderson's Relish before adding the stock and bringing to the boil. Reduce the heat and simmer gently for 1½ hours.

Preheat the oven to 190°c.

Place the filling mixture in an ovenproof dish. Line the rim with a thin strip of pastry and brush with beaten egg.

Roll out a piece of pastry as big as the dish and place it on top, then press the edges together to seal. If you wish, decorate your pie with pastry trimmings.

Make a steam hole in the centre using a sharp knife, then brush with more beaten egg.

Transfer to the oven and cook for 1-1½ hours. If the pastry gets too brown, cover it with foil.

Serve hot with beef gravy and add a little Henderson's Relish for extra flavour.

# *Derbyshire pride*
# ITALIAN INSPIRATION

Experienced chef, Chris Mapp, has worked all over the country with many top chefs including Marcus Wareing, Gordon Ramsay and Paul Ainsworth – but his heart has always been at home in Derbyshire.

Chris Mapp, chef and restaurateur behind Barlow's Tickled Trout, boasts an impressive culinary background.

He has worked at London's Pétrus with Marcus Wareing and Gordon Ramsay, the Greenhouse in Mayfair, and set up Padstow's No. 6 with Paul Ainsworth. But he couldn't resist the call of his home village when his favourite local came up for sale.

Opened in August 2014, The Tickled Trout has been a breath of fresh air for Barlow. Chris has turned a run-down pub into a relaxed, cosmopolitan space with bar, restaurant, lounge and an airy conservatory, offering appealing spaces all year round - for drinkers and diners alike.

'Derbyshire Pride, Italian Inspiration' is the restaurant's motto.

Italian influence is rippled throughout the menu in dishes including sourdough pizzas, lamb meatballs, and a charcuterie sharing board. But they are all made using Derbyshire produce: meat from Highfield House Farm, rapeseed oil from

Brock & Morten, cured meats from Jaquest in Bolsover, ice cream from Bradwell's and dairy produce from Woodthorpe Grange Farm in Tupton.

Attention to detail is key and everything is made from scratch where possible. Nothing is done by halves. Beef is slow-cooked overnight for Sunday roasts; burgers are made from two different cuts; all meats except beef are brined for a juicier, flavoursome finish; fish is caught and delivered the same day from Cornwall.

A daily specials board sits alongside the à la carte, showcasing seasonal ingredients, and Sunday roasts are served family-style, with bowls of veg to get stuck into and all the trimmings.

Service is paramount. Chris has put together an impressive front-of-house team led by Tom Schofield who guarantees a warm welcome, while Mark Taylor and Tom Alberts head up the kitchen.

There is a private dining room upstairs to seat 30, where diners can enjoy tailored menus if they wish; it is popular for celebrations, business meetings and private dinners.

...enu
...aturday 12-2.30pm

...d Cornish trout, almonds, pancetta lardons
and herbed gnocchi                                    £15·95

...ne, tomato and mozzarella bake, rocket
Salad and pesto bread                                 £12·00

...k and ale pie with roasted root                     £13·95

...nzola picante pizza                                 £12·75

# The Tickled Trout
# CORNISH SEA TROUT

With almonds, pancetta lardons, herbed gnocchi. Serves 4.

## Ingredients

4 sea trout fillets (ask your fishmonger to scale, de-bone and score the skin)

2 tbsp smoked bacon or pancetta lardons

3-4 large carrots, peeled and cut into batons

1 punnet French beans, trimmed

2 tbsp flaked almonds, toasted

50g butter, cubed

100ml chicken or vegetable stock

2 tsp chopped chives and chervil

Olive oil

200g baked potato flesh

4 free range egg yolks

60g '00' flour, plus extra for rolling

30g Parmesan, freshly grated

1 tsp salt

2 tsp fresh marjoram, chopped

## Method

Preheat the oven to 180°c.

Bake the potatoes for 1 hour, or until cooked through. Remove from the oven and set aside to cool. Cut the potatoes in half and scoop 200g of the flesh into a bowl. Discard the skins.

Mash through a ricer until smooth and add the egg yolks, flour, Parmesan, salt and marjoram. Stir until the mixture comes together as a dough.

Divide the mixture into four, then on a floured surface roll each piece into a long sausage shape, about 1¼cm in diameter.

Cut each sausage into 2½cm pieces of gnocchi – each gnocchi will look like a small pillow.

Bring a large saucepan of salted water to the boil. Drop the gnocchi in and cook for 1-2 minutes, or until they float, then drop them into icy water.

Blanch the French beans and carrots by dropping into salted boiling water for 3-4 minutes, then into iced water. Then repeat the process with the lardons but use unsalted water, this is to remove the excess salt from the lardons.

In a pan heat up a little oil. When warm add the trout fillets one at a time, skin-side down, and gently hold with your fingers so the fish doesn't curl up. Cook on a medium heat to lightly colour the skin – do not turn over.

In another pan heat a little more oil and add the lardons. When the fat has started to colour and the bacon is starting to crisp add a couple of cubes of butter. Stir in the gnocchi to give it a little colour.

When the butter has melted, add a small amount of stock and stir. Allow the liquid to reduce by half on a medium heat to create an emulsion to nicely coat the vegetables.

Add the toasted almonds and vegetables and check the seasoning.

By now the trout will almost be cooked – you will see that the colour of the flesh has changed and is paler apart from the fattest part. Turn the fillets over and cook for 1 more minute.

Now add the chopped herbs to the pan with the vegetables and stir. Pour onto your tray to remove excess liquid then portion between your bowls, putting the gnocchi around the edges and the rest in the middle.

Sit the trout fillets on top of the carrots and beans in the middle of the bowl and serve immediately.

# The Tickled Trout
## POACHED PEACHES

With light peach gelée, apricot marmalade, sorbet, popcorn. Serves 4-6.
The beauty of this dish is that you can have all the elements prepared
before your guests arrive.

## Ingredients

**For the stock syrup:**

300ml water

225g caster sugar

**For the apricot sorbet:**

500g apricot purée

150ml stock syrup

50g water

1 vanilla pod, split and de-seeded

**For the poached peaches:**

800g peaches, halves

1.2 litres water

200g caster sugar

**For the peach gelée:**

300ml peach jus (the liquid the peaches were poached in)

2 leaves gelatine

**For the apricot marmalade:**

900g fresh apricots, halved

100g caster sugar

2 vanilla pod, split and de-seeded

½ lemongrass stick

**For the caramelised popcorn:**

200g sugar

40g popcorn

Small knob of butter

## Method

**To make a stock syrup (for the sorbet)**

Combine the water and caster sugar in a pan, stir together and bring to the boil, then take off the heat.

**For the sorbet**

Combine all the ingredients and churn in an ice cream machine until thickened. Keep in the freezer until required.

**For the poached peaches**

Cover the peach halves with the water and sugar and bring to the boil. Once at boiling point remove from the heat and allow to cool in the hot liquid.

Once cool cut the peach halves into 6-8 slices each, depending on size, and fan them out in two 10cm metal pastry rings in a shallow bowl – this is what you will be serving the dish in. Place in the fridge and keep the remaining poaching liquor.

**To make the gelée**

Soak the gelatine leaves in cold water until soft and squeeze out excess water. Take around 50ml of the poaching liquor, bring to the boil and remove from the heat. Whisk in the gelatine then add the remaining liquor.

Put the gelée in the fridge to begin the setting process – do not leave too long as it needs to be semi-set. Once semi-set, pour the gelée over the peaches up to the rim of the pastry ring. Return to the fridge to set.

**For the marmalade**

Combine all the ingredients and slowly reduce on a medium heat to your desired consistency. If you think it has reduced too far, you can add a little water to loosen it. Once the gelée has set in the fridge, spoon a small amount of the marmalade in the centres of the fans of peaches.

**For the popcorn**

Take the sugar to golden caramel in a heavy based pan – do not stir or it may crystallise. Once golden, stir in the popcorn using a wooden spoon. Drop in a small knob of butter and pour onto a tray lined with baking paper.

**To serve**

Run a small knife around the rings to free them from the gelée. Pour a little of the remaining poaching liquor around the set peaches and place 4-5 pieces of caramelised popcorn around the edges. Scoop a ball of sorbet on to the marmalade and serve.

*Tip: For the photo Chris used normal peaches, but for a better taste and effect white peaches are the perfect choice when they are in season in the summer.*

# Sally Pepper's
## SAUSAGE SURPRISE

Sally Pepper is a Derbyshire lass – she was born in Belper, lived in Shirland and went to school in Alfreton – but after graduating with a theatre degree from Leeds University, she headed for the 'Big Smoke' to find fame and fortune.

While performing in a play on the London Fringe, a fellow actress suggested she audition as a broadcast travel news presenter, and a few days later Sally was offered the job.

Sally has worked as a radio and TV presenter for commercial channels and the BBC over the last 17 years and currently presents a show every weekday on BBC Radio Derby.

Her love of food started when she helped her Mum with the baking – and licking the bowl (still her favourite part!). She is now passing that cookery knowledge on to her two young sons who have helped her to create this dish.

Food for Sally is a sociable experience, be it sitting around the dinner table with the family or spending a relaxing evening with friends.

With this dish the preparation is done beforehand – meaning you can stick it in the oven and enjoy the wine and conversation until it's ready. It works equally as a winter warmer or as a twist for a summer's evening barbecue. Serves 4.

## Ingredients

1 tbsp olive oil

2 red onions

2 carrots

2 parsnips

2 yellow peppers

8 sausages – I use New Yorker sausages from pork reared by Rachel Frearson at Potlocks Farm in Radbourne

½ orange, juice and zest

2 tsp heather honey – mine is from the Honey Pot at Markeaton Park, Derby

1 sprig rosemary

## Method

Heat the oven to 200°c (180°c for fan oven).

Chop the vegetables into chunks and place in a roasting tin. Drizzle the oil over and toss together. Cook in the oven for 10 minutes.

Give the vegetables a shake then place the sausages on top and bake for a further 10 minutes.

Meanwhile, mix the honey, orange zest and juice together.

Pour this over the sausages and vegetables, sprinkle the rosemary over and bake for a further 15 minutes.

Serve with creamy cheesy mash or dauphinoise potatoes and wash it down with a glass of Merlot. Cheers!

*Tip: My New Yorker sausages included chilli, paprika and fennel, but the joy of this dish is you can use any flavour sausage – that's the surprise!*

# Brewing
# DERBYSHIRE

The beating heart of the UK brewing scene, Derbyshire is undoubtedly a beer enthusiast's dream destination.
From micro to massive, bottles to barrels, the region is positively teeming with knowledgeable, forward thinking producers – offering a wide range of stunning ales.
Here, we take a look at four of the finest...

# A pint short
# OF A FIRKIN

The success of Thornbridge Brewery is nothing short of phenomenal.
A host of top awards has secured their premier place in the
British brewing industry.

Thornbridge is a multi-award-winning brewery nestled amid the scenic landscape of the Peak District National Park.

Producing over 100,000 pints of beer a week, and holding a wealth of acclaim including BBC Drinks Producer of the Year 2014, the brewery has firmly established itself as a key player in the British brewing industry.

In fact, the brewery has around 400 awards, and with World Beer Cup and World Beer medals to their name one might arrive at the notion that world dominance was always on the cards.

But tell that to business partners Jim Harrison and Simon Webster back in 2004 when they were recruiting a young professional brewing team and setting up the brewery in outbuildings at Jim's family home, Thornbridge Hall, and they'd have thought you were a pint short of a firkin.

Their big breakthrough came in June 2005, with the arrival of what is now their flagship beer, Jaipur – a hoppy, 5.9% India Pale Ale. A win at that year's Sheffield CAMRA beer festival was the catalyst for a whole host of accolades, leading to high demand for Thornbridge's innovative beers.

With this breakthrough award and increasing demand for Thornbridge beers, Simon and Jim took steps to grow the brewery. Additional brewers were brought on board and a decision was taken that would determine the brewery's future – remain a small ten-barrel plant or start looking for a new, bigger location.

The latter won out – and brewing moved to Bakewell's Riverside Business Park, just a stone's throw from the Hall. A £2million state-of-the-art brewery was commissioned and large-scale production began in September 2009. More awards followed – and Thornbridge beers became regulars on the shelves of Waitrose stores nationwide.

Big sellers, such as Jaipur, Tzara and Halcyon, are brewed daily at Riverside – while the smaller brewery at the Hall has been retained for bespoke runs, giving the brewers another outlet to experiment and implement their creative flair.

The diversity of Thornbridge's beers is of great appeal. Inventive brews using ingredients from cucumber to pumpkin, to peanuts and chocolate have been conceived, as well as collaborations with other breweries and producers.

Thornbridge now operates on a global scale, from Bakewell to Brooklyn, producing in excess of six million pints a year, with around 20 per cent of that exported overseas to more than 30 countries.

They are still firmly rooted in the Peak District and this, coupled with expansion, is demonstrative of their focus on growing while retaining the quality, innovation, passion and knowledge they are known for.

The brewery is a friendly place, in a picturesque setting, especially when bathed in sunshine and blue skies. Music streams from the building's shining steel innards and there's a general air of cheeriness. Members of the public are welcome to experience this themselves on a guided tour, which runs twice a week on Wednesday and Friday afternoons.

As well as their online outlet, there is also a shop on site, which is the best place to pick up a range of Thornbridge's beers and other merchandise. There are plans to expand and create a visitor centre called The Barrel Room, where beer-lovers can shop, learn and experience Thornbridge's developing barrel ageing projects.

They are further encouraged to get involved at Thornbridge's range of local pubs via art and music events, as well as their annual summer festival, The Great Peak Weekender.

Thornbridge reached the grand old age of ten in 2015 and began its celebrations with a special 10% edition Jaipur X. And, while it might be one of the more established of the new wave of British craft breweries, there's a feeling the surface has only been scratched. Keep a close eye on these guys...

# Born to BREW

With the desire to produce great beer, Kim Beresford and Roy Shorrock have taken the Ashover Brewery from a dream to reality.

Ashover Brewery was founded by publican Kim Beresford and former Chesterfield CAMRA chairman Roy Shorrock in 2007.

Kim had previously been a passionate home brewer. He had harboured a wish of starting his own brewery for sometime.

Meanwhile, Roy was also on the lookout for a pastime related to his love of beer following his early retirement from the IT industry.

The two beer enthusiasts discovered their shared ambition while chatting over a pint in Kim's pub, The Old Poets' Corner at Ashover.

They initially considered installing a brewery in the pub's basement, but on discovering this wasn't viable, they started looking for another location. It was shortly afterwards that the cottage adjoining the pub – originally its coaching stables – came up for sale and the perfect space presented itself.

Roy quickly set to work sourcing equipment, which ended up coming all the way from the north of Scotland. The disused

kit had previously been used at The Rocket in Crawley, which became the Firecracker and Firkin, before it went to the Rat & Ratchet in Huddersfield, then on to Fantasy Brewery in Nuneaton.

Kim and Roy first brewed in January 2007 on their four barrel plant – the equivalent to around 16 firkins or 1,152 pints at a time – with advice from Titanic Brewery's founder Keith Bott, who lives locally.

Roy's daughter, Janine, joined them from the beginning in her free time, but as the brewery's reputation flourished, she gave up her office job to become Ashover's full time and only brewer.

Kim knew from the outset what beers he wanted the brewery to produce based on a popular range served in his pub. Ashover now has a core range inspired by the local area, including Poets' Tipple, a traditional 4% bitter. Light Rale, a pale 3.7% session beer, Littlemoor Citra, an American hopped pale ale 4.1%, and Coffin Lane Stout at 5%.

Some beers are dictated by the seasons, such as Porters brewed with locally picked damsons, plums and blackcurrants, and the very popular Elderflower, a 4% pale beer for which a team of pickers forage around 12 kilos of fresh, local elderflowers.

Every year in September, Janine also brews a 'green hopped' beer, using freshly harvested hops grown and picked in Chesterfield by John Pople, local horticulturist. All the spent hops from the brewery are used by local allotments as an excellent source of fertiliser.

Unsurprisingly, some of Ashover's creations have become award-winners, with accolades from SIBA and CAMRA. The brewery has won the CAMRA East Midlands region competition three times in the last five years with Poets' Tipple and Hydro. This in turn put them into the national competition, which considers the top 50 beers in the country out of around 10,000.

The brewery supplies around 20 pubs, mainly in the local area, including Kim's Codnor pub, The Poet & Castle. Janine also hand bottles small batches of an ever changing variety of bottle conditioned beers. Beer connoisseurs can pick these up from specialist shops in Derbyshire.

There is also the opportunity to try a wide selection of Ashover's brews at the twice-annual, Old Poets' Corner beer festival, which has been running for over a decade. The festival showcases 15 guest ales and a range of ciders at any one time – and goes through around 50 different beers across the event weekend.

With Kim looking after the pubs, Roy in charge of sales and deliveries and Janine brewing award-winning beers, this trio proves that the best things really do come in small packages.

# At the Peak of THEIR CRAFT

From a garage, to a purpose built brewery – the rise of Buxton Brewery
has been nothing short of meteoric.

Climbing enthusiast Geoff Quinn moved to Buxton just over a decade ago to take advantage of the Peak District's rocky outcrops when he wasn't at work in his IT role.

His other hobby was home brewing and observation of the UK craft beer revival. This, coupled with a desire to be his own boss, got Geoff thinking.

More used to leaping around a rock face, Geoff took a leap of faith in business, and on New Year's Day 2009 he set up Buxton Brewery in his garage with some second-hand equipment. Fast forward a year, and running the brewery became Geoff's full-time job.

The brewery relocated to Buxton's Staden Business Park in January 2010 and expanded further in 2013 to a purpose-built 32 hectolitre plant, increasing brewing capacity more than four-fold. As well as gaining popularity in the British market, Buxton now exports around half its produce to over 20 countries including Italy, Spain and Brazil.

Geoff works closely with brewery manager Denis Johnstone and head brewer Colin Stronge, who previously spent nine years at Manchester's Marble Brewery. Buxton has become known for its hoppy, strong IPAs and pale ales, but boasts a range of styles from imperial stouts to sour beers, porters and more.

They are currently focusing on their barrel ageing programme and experimenting with different yeasts to change taste and aroma. American bourbon barrels are a favourite and wine barrels have also been used in creative wood-aged brews, allowing the beer to absorb a spectrum of flavours.

Many of Buxton's beers are named after popular local climbing spots such as the well-known IPA Axe Edge and India Red Ale High Tor, while the brewery logo features Buxton landmark Solomon's Temple, a Victorian fortified hill marker on the edge of the town.

With 40 different beers brewed last year, a handful of collaborations with international breweries and a third year in the top 100 breweries in the world on public-voted site ratebeer.com, Buxton Brewery is well worth getting acquainted with.

# The Peak of
# PERFECTION

Peak Ales' future looks rosy with expansion to an all new brewery and plenty of bespoke brews on the cards.

It was Rob Evans' impending 40th birthday that made him turn to beer. Brewing, in fact.

He and wife Debra had toyed with the idea of starting their own business after becoming disillusioned with the world of teaching.

A cask ale enthusiast, Rob signed up to learn the brewing trade at Cannon Royall Brewery, in the back of a pub near Worcester.

Then, combining these skills with knowledge from brewing courses at Sunderland University and from established consultant David Smith, he set about establishing a brewery of his own.

Recognising a gap in the market, the Evans' moved to Rob's native Derbyshire, knowing they would need help from the family. After a couple of potential sites fell through, Rob approached the Chatsworth estate, which had an ideal barn on the Baslow Road.

Funding and planning eventually lined up, but plans were once again delayed after a resident family of barn owls was discovered – Rob and Debra endured another agonising wait until their feathered guests vacated.

Finally, in February 2005, Peak Ales' 10-barrel plant produced its first brew.

Core beers are Swift Nick, a session beer with a fruit and hop aroma; Bakewell Best Bitter, an amber ale; and Chatsworth Gold, a slightly stronger golden beer made using Chatsworth estate honey.

Seasonal brews include blonde beer Summer Sovereign and the autumnal Paxton, a full-bodied ruby red ale.

Rob has worked with colleagues Stuart Wragg, Michael Robinson, Thom Bettney and Tom Neale to achieve Peak Ales' success – and satisfy a range of thirsts.

The brewers are supported by Debra in the office, as well as Eloise Hopkinson, Louise Rhodes and Dave Spencer.

And the future looks rosy. Demand has led to expansion as Peak Ales recently opened a new 20-barrel plant at Ashford-in-the-Water. The barn brewery will become a visitors' centre, housing a small micro-brewery for bespoke brews and to enable the public to learn about the brewing process.

Peak Ales' beers can be found in a variety of Peak District pubs and local independent beer shops.

# Peak Ales
# CHATSWORTH GOLD ALE MUSTARD

Makes one small jar.
Served with a stunning belly pork dish from Riley's of Bakewell.

## Ingredients

100g whole yellow mustard seeds

15g plain flour

2 tsp fine sea salt

175ml Chatsworth Gold Ale

## Method

Grind the mustard seeds to a smooth powder using either an electric spice grinder or coffee grinder.

Transfer the ground seeds to a bowl and add the flour and salt.

Gradually whisk in the ale until it takes on a smooth, creamy consistency.

Spoon the mustard into sterilised glass jars and secure with well-fitting lids.

Leave to mature for at least two weeks in a cool place before tasting.

# The DIRECTORY

These great businesses have supported the making of this book; please support and enjoy them.

**Anoki**
129 London Road,
Derby DE1 2QN
Telephone: 01332 292888
Website: www.anoki.co.uk
*Anoki fine dining Indian restaurant gives diners a true taste of the sub-continent, with its lavishly decorated interiors, authentic recipes and traditionally dressed waiting staff.*

**The Apple Tree Gift Shop and Teahouse**
6 Flood Street,
Ockbrook,
Derby DE72 3RF
Telephone: 01332 987001
Website:
www.theappletreegiftshop.co.uk
*Quintessential teahouse serving light lunches and homemade cakes complemented by the gift shop where you can find beautiful cards, jewellery and gifts.*

**Ashover Brewery**
Butts Road,
Ashover,
Chesterfield,
Derbyshire S45 0EW
Telephone: 07803 708526 /
07976 574361
Website: www.ashoverbrewery.co.uk
*Ashover brewery has been producing award-winning, hand crafted beers in Derbyshire since 2007.*

**Baked artisan bakery and café**
16 The Strand,
Derby DE1 1BE
Telephone: 01332 346804
Twitter: @BAKEDderby
*Baked is an artisan bakery and café serving fresh homemade food made from scratch and great tasting coffee and tea.*

**The Bakewell Bakery**
Unit 14,
Riverside Business Park,
Bakewell,
Derbyshire DE45 1GS
Telephone: 01629 814996
Website: www.thebakewellbakery.co.uk
*Bakewell based bakery selling homemade bread and confectionary. Suppliers of the famous Original Bakewell Pudding.*

**Bakewell Cookshop**
10 Matlock Street,
Bakewell,
Derbyshire DE45 1EE
Telephone: 01629 812620
Website: www.bakewellcookshop.com
*Sellers of design led kitchen gifts and essentials, at the heart of the Peak District.*

**The Barrel Inn**
Bretton,
Near Eyam,
Hope Valley S32 5QD
Telephone: 01433 630856
Website: www.thebarrelinn.co.uk
*The highest pub in Derbyshire with panoramic views of the county, serving home cooked traditional fare and fine ales.*

**Bean Caffé**
Friar Gate Studios,
Ford Street,
Derby DE1 1EE
Telephone: 01332 258318
Website: www.beancaffe.co.uk
*Creative, friendly café offering fresh homemade breakfast, lunch and brunch.*

**Brock & Morten**

Highfield Farm,

Ashford in the Water,

Bakewell,

Derbyshire DE45 1QN

Telephone: 07739 188111

Website: www.brockandmorten.com

*Cold pressed rapeseed oil producers.*

**The Bulls Head Monyash**

Church Street,

Monyash,

Bakewell,

Derbyshire DE45 1JH

Telephone: 01629 812372

Website:

www.thebullsheadmonyash.co.uk

*Traditional public house with a modern flair restaurant.*

**Buxton Brewery Company Ltd**

Staden Business Park,

Buxton,

Derbyshire SK17 9RZ

Telephone: 01298 244200

Website: www.buxtonbrewery.co.uk

*Craft micro-brewery in Buxton, Derbyshire.*

**Buxton Tap House**

The Old Courthouse,

George Street,

Buxton,

Derbyshire SK17 6AT

Telephone: 01298 214085

Website: www.buxtontaphouse.co.uk

*15 Buxton beers on draft, 80+ world beers, wines and spirits, smoked food specialists.*

**Chatsworth Estate Farm Shop**

Pilsley,

Bakewell,

Derbyshire DE45 1UF

Telephone: 01246 565400

Website: www.chatsworth.org

*Chatsworth Estate Farm Shop prides itself on providing estate and locally sourced produce.*

**Denby Pottery**

Denby Retail Ltd,

Denby,

Derbyshire DE5 8NX

Telephone: 01773 740722

Website: www.denby.co.uk

*Established in 1809 Denby has been making superior tableware and pottery in the English countryside for over two hundred years.*

**Derby Tourist Information Centre**

Assembly Rooms,

Market Place,

Derby DE1 3AH

Telephone: 01332 643411

Website: www.visitderby.co.uk

*For all you need to know about Derby and the surrounding area, visit Derby Tourist Information Centre for the latest information, local souvenirs, ticket sales and advice.*

**The Devonshire Arms**

Devonshire Square,

Beeley, Chatsworth Estate,

Derbyshire DE4 2NR

Telephone: 01629 733259

Website: www.devonshirebeeley.co.uk

*Set in the stunning scenery of the Derbyshire Peak District and just a short walk away from the wonderful Chatsworth House and Gardens The Devonshire Arms at Beeley is a picturesque country inn with a contemporary Brasserie restaurant.*

**The Devonshire Arms**

Pilsley, Chatsworth Estate,

Derbyshire DE45 1UL

Telephone: 01246 583258

Website: www.devonshirepilsley.co.uk

*A traditional inn, serving up a mix of warm hospitality, good pub food and Peak District real ales.*

**Eroica Britannia**

The Showground

Bakewell, Derbyshire DE45 1AQ

Website: www.eroicabritannia.co.uk

*An iconic family friendly festival setting up camp in Bakewell, held in June annually.*

**Fischer's at Baslow Hall**

Calver Road,

Baslow, Derbyshire DE45 1RR

Telephone: 01246 583259

Website:

www.fischers-baslowhall.co.uk

*Michelin starred restaurant with rooms. Stylishly tranquil, fabulously friendly and something a little different.*

**Hide Burger Bar**

Riverside Chambers,

Derwent Street,

Derby DE1 2EP

Telephone: 07572 296870

Website: www.hideburgerbar.co.uk

*A burger bar with a small simple burger menu made from good honest ingredients, inspired by not just British food, but by local produce too.*

**Iberico World Tapas Derby**

9-11 Bold Lane,

Derby DE1 3NT

Telephone: 01332 345456

Website: www.ibericotapas.com

*Iberico World Tapas combines the rustic simplicity of Spanish Tapas with the refined ingredients of world cooking.*

**Losehill House Hotel and Spa**
Lose Hill Lane,
Edale Road,
Hope,
Derbyshire S33 6AF
Telephone: 01433 621219
Website www.losehillhouse.co.uk
*Fine hotel and spa in the Peak District National Park, with one of the most highly regarded restaurants in Derbyshire.*

**Marketing Derby**
Riverside Chambers,
Full Street,
Derby DE1 3AF
Telephone: 01332 201860
Website: www.marketingderby.co.uk
*Marketing Derby is funded by Derby City Council and over 250 of the city's businesses, who are bondholders, with the aim of supporting and attracting investment to the city.*

**Marsh Green Farm Shop**
Matlock Road,
Kelstedge,
Nr Chesterfield,
Derbyshire S45 0DX
Telephone: 01246 591516
Website:
www.marshgreenfarmshop.co.uk
*Farm shop, café and deli.*

**Matlock Meadows Ltd**
Masson Farm,
Snitterton Rd,
Matlock,
Derbyshire DE4 2JG
Telephone: 01629 760596
Website: www.matlockmeadows.co.uk
*Italian style ice cream handmade on the working dairy farm in the heart of the Derbyshire Dales countryside.*

**Morley Hayes**
Main Road,
Morley,
Derbyshire DE7 6DG
Telephone: 01332 780480
Website: www.morleyhayes.com
*Luxury four star hotel with prestigious Dovecote Restaurant amidst beautiful Derbyshire countryside.*

**Nonnas Chesterfield Ltd**
131 Chatsworth Road,
Chesterfield,
Derbyshire S40 2AH
Telephone: 01246 380035
Website: www.nonnas.co.uk
*Contemporary restaurant offering Italian hospitality, food and wine since 2009.*

**Nourish at No. 44**
44 King Street,
Belper,
Derbyshire DE56 1PL
Telephone: 01773 824480
Website: www.nourishatno44.co.uk
*Licensed independent bistro serving fresh, locally sourced ingredients, classic French and traditional British dishes with a modern twist.*

**The Old Bakewell Pudding Shop**
The Square,
Bakewell,
Derbyshire DE45 1BT
Telephone: 01629 812193
Website:
www.bakewellpuddingshop.co.uk
*Home of the Bakewell pudding, a local deli and restaurant serving lunches and cream teas.*

**The Old Hall Inn
& The Paper Mill Inn**
Whitehough,
Chinley,
High Peak,
Derbyshire SK23 6EJ
Telephone: 01663 750529
Website: www.old-hall-inn.co.uk
*Two award-winning ale houses serving fantastic food in the heart of the Peak District.*

**The Old Poets Corner**
Butts Road,
Ashover,
Chesterfield,
Derbyshire S45 0EW
Telephone: 01246 590888
Website: www.oldpoets.co.uk
*A traditional English rural village pub with hop-adorned beams and log fires, real ale to die for, wholesome fresh cooked food, and beautiful en-suite rooms.*

**Opulence Restaurant at Cathedral Quarter Hotel**
16 Saint Mary's Gate,
Derby DE1 3JR
Telephone: 01332 546080
Website:
www.cathedralquarterhotel.com
*Upscale restaurant serving modern British food in elegant surroundings.*

**Owen Taylor & Sons Ltd**
27 Main Road,
Leabrooks,
Alfreton,
Derbyshire DE55 1LA
Telephone: 01773 603351 /
01773 600007
Website: www.owentaylor.co.uk
*Catering and wholesale butchers supplying Derbyshire and the East Midlands with both traditional and innovative meats and meat products.*

**The Packhorse Inn**

Packhorse Inn,
Main Street,
Little Longstone,
Bakewell,
Derbyshire DE45 1TA
Telephone: 01629 640471
Website:
www.packhorselongstone.co.uk
*Situated just off the Monsal Trail, this historic pub is surrounded by some of the most striking scenery the Peaks have to offer. The perfect setting to enjoy real ales and locally sourced food.*

**Peak Ales**

The Barn Brewery,
Chatsworth,
Bakewell,
Derbyshire DE45 1EX
Telephone: 01246 583737
Website: www.peakales.co.uk
*Craft ales traditionally brewed on the Chatsworth Estate in the Peak District.*

**The Plough Inn**

Matlock Road,
Brackenfield,
Alfreton,
Derbyshire DE55 6DD
Telephone: 01629 534437
Website:
www.ploughinnbrackenfield.co.uk
*Country pub serving traditional pub classics and modern British cuisine.*

**Pointing Dog & Duck**

Rutland Mill, Coombs Rd,
Bakewell,
Derbyshire DE45 1AQ
Telephone: 01629 813813
Website: www.pointingdog.co.uk
*Standing on the banks of the River Wye in Bakewell for daily dining and drinking and special occasions.*

**Rowley's of Baslow**

Church Lane,
Baslow,
Derbyshire DE45 1RY
Telephone: 01246 583880
Website: www.rowleysrestaurant.co.uk
*Fresh, seasonal food using local ingredients in an informal and relaxed atmosphere.*

**Samuel Fox Country Inn**

Stretfield Road,
Bradwell,
Hope Valley S33 9JT
Telephone: 01433 621562
Website: www.samuelfox.co.uk
*Pub dining at its very best; stunning food, fine wines, real ale, a relaxed atmosphere and a warm welcome in the beautiful Hope Valley.*

**The Scotsman's Pack**

School Lane,
Hathersage,
Hope Valley S32 1BZ
Telephone: 01433 650253
Website: www.scotsmanspack.com
*Traditional country pub with rooms with an established reputation for quality meals and friendly service.*

**Thornbridge Brewery**

Riverside Brewery,
Buxton Road,
Bakewell,
Derbyshire DE45 1GS
Telephone: 01629 815999
Website:
www.thornbridgebrewery.co.uk
*Britain's most awarded brewery making beer with innovation, passion and knowledge in the heart of the Peak District.*

**The Tickled Trout**

33 Valley Road,
Barlow,
Derbyshire S18 7SL
Telephone: 0114 2891111
Website: www.tickledtroutbarlow.com
*Proud of Derbyshire and inspired by Italy. Using the finest locally sourced ingredients to create delicious food with an Italian twist in a modern, contemporary and friendly environment.*

# The INDEX